Trilogy Christian Publishers
A Wholly Owned Subsidiary of Trinity Broadcasting Network
2442 Michelle Drive
Tustin, CA 92780

Copyright © 2024 by Vadim Makoyed

Scripture quotations marked AMPCE are taken from the Amplified Bible, Copyright © 1954, 1958, 1962, 1964, 1965, 1987 by The Lockman Foundation. Used by permission. Scripture quotations marked ESV are taken from the ESV® Bible (The Holy Bible, English Standard Version®), copyright © 2001 by Crossway Bibles, a publishing ministry of Good News Publishers. Used by permission. All rights reserved. Scripture quotations marked NASB are taken from the New American Standard Bible® (NASB), Copyright © 1960, 1962, 1963, 1968, 1971, 1972, 1973, 1975, 1977, 1995 by The Lockman Foundation. Used by permission. www.Lockman.org. Scripture quotations marked NCV are taken from the New Century Version®. Copyright © 2005 by Thomas Nelson. Used by permission. All rights reserved. Scripture quotations marked NIV are taken from the Holy Bible, New International Version®, NIV®. Copyright © 1973, 1978, 1984, 2011 by Biblica, Inc.TM Used by permission of Zondervan. All rights reserved worldwide. www.zondervan.com. The "NIV" and "New International Version" are trademarks registered in the United States Patent and Trademark Office by Biblica, Inc.TM. Scripture quotations marked NKJV are taken from the New King James Version®. Copyright © 1982 by Thomas Nelson. Used by permission. All rights reserved. Scripture quotations marked TPT are from The Passion Translation®. Copyright © 2017, 2018 by Passion & Fire Ministries, Inc. Used by permission. All rights reserved. ThePassionTranslation.com. Scripture quotations marked KJV are taken from the King James Version of the Bible. Public domain.

All rights reserved, including the right to reproduce this book or portions thereof in any form whatsoever. For information, address Trilogy Christian Publishing

Rights Department, 2442 Michelle Drive, Tustin, CA 92780.
Trilogy Christian Publishing/TBN and colophon are trademarks of Trinity Broadcasting Network.
For information about special discounts for bulk purchases, please contact Trilogy Christian Publishing.

Trilogy Disclaimer: The views and content expressed in this book are those of the author and may not necessarily reflect the views and doctrine of Trilogy Christian Publishing or the Trinity Broadcasting Network.

10 9 8 7 6 5 4 3 2 1
Library of Congress Cataloging-in-Publication Data is available.
ISBN 979-8-89041-734-3
ISBN 979-8-89041-735-0 (e-book)

DEDICATION

I dedicate this book to my wife, Natalie. I am always amazed at how your unconditional love finds a way to do good around you. You are my bride, showing by example how to live worthy of this status with Jesus.

ACKNOWLEDGMENTS

I want to thank my wife for being the first one to inspire me to write this book. I thank my parents for their unconditional support. I thank the nameless and the faceless men and women I get to pray with weekly.

CONTENTS

Introduction	9
♦ ANTICIPATING JESUS	**13**
The End Begins with Faith	15
Old Testament Jesus	21
The First Church Anticipated Jesus	35
The Bride Anticipates Jesus	41
Does the Modern Church Anticipate Jesus?	55
♦ LETTERS TO THE MODERN CHURCH	**73**
To the Comfortable Church	75
To the Foolish Church	87
To the Obese Church	109
To the Sleeping Church	129
To the Barren Church	155
To the Corrupt Church	173
♦ READY OR NOT	**193**
The Beginning of the End	195
Revival Lifestyle	211
Endnotes	215

INTRODUCTION

THERE IS A REMNANT OF CHRISTIANS. They are a different kind of believers. They stand out among their peers with a vibrant, unceasing, vigilant desire—to get ready for the coming Bridegroom.

They are the Bride living by standards and commitment on a different level. These Christians are uncompromising, incorruptible, and impossible to seduce. This Bride is a remnant of the believers whom Jesus will marry one day.

It may have been a while, but the day will surely come when the Bride in love with the Bridegroom will unite in marriage and be together for all eternity. These believers are engaged to the Lamb of God.

Unfortunately, a great apostasy has come against the church like a sneaky snake in the garden. In this subtle game, the church had slowly fallen for the familiar voice that sounds identical to the truth, yet it is not.

Jesus had a word war with the devil back in the desert (Matthew 4:1–11). While wiped out from a forty-day fast, Jesus had to fight His own words, shot His way by the enemy. How does one fight Bible verses with Bible verses? What does one do when the enemy quotes the truth? Maybe he's not the enemy if he knows Christ so well. Maybe he is the biggest fan. In response, Jesus struck to the heart. He could not be manipulated and cheated. He saw the cunning lies and overcame them.

Sadly, the modern church is not winning this battle. The church knows the Bible well but not the heart behind it.

The craftiness of the enemy seduced the modern church. She fell away from the true image Jesus envisioned when He created her. The church is not ready for the wedding, and the time is running out. We live in the end times, and Jesus is coming like a thief at night. It is time to get ready quickly.

I wrote this book to help us prepare. I challenge the reader to examine many areas of our Christian lives that may cause us to be not ready as the Bride—individually and as a church body.

"The time is come that judgement must begin at the house of God" (1 Peter 4:17, KJV).

Like a text message that can come off wrong, I hope you don't get the wrong idea, but you can feel my heart in this longer text. I love you, and I love the church. The church is one of my deepest passions and burdens. I do not want to sugarcoat anything but write it like it is in a very candid way.

As Martin Luther said, "Let me rather speak the truth with too great severity than once to act the hypocrite and conceal the truth."

Some may think that I am too negative and critical in this book. Some may even think that I am anti-church. But I am reminded of Jeremiah, who prophesied to Israel that they would be destroyed, go into captivity, and be exiled to Babylon. The people accused him of being anti-Israel. They claimed he hated the Jewish people for speaking such a negative message.

No one cared to know that Jeremiah would go home to cry and weep for the nation unwilling to repent. "Oh, that my head were waters, and my eyes a fountain of tears, That I might weep day and night For the slain of the daughter of my people!" (Jeremiah 9:1, ESV).

INTRODUCTION

I, too, cry for the modern church because she went astray too far away from the cross. It is a complex subject to discuss, so I put it aside for a long time until the Holy Spirit cornered me, telling me to start writing. I would instead write about something positive and uplifting. It is much safer. But the Word of God is not primarily for that. It is "for doctrine, for reproof, for correction, for instruction in righteousness" (2 Timothy 3:16, KJV).

Leonard Ravenhill writes, "Where is our heartbreak over the malignancies that bind our people today? When, oh, when did your pastor cry in a fervent prayer from the pulpit, 'Oh, that You would rend the heavens! That You would come down!'"[1]

So, open your heart and let the Word of God do its precise, detailed, surgical work. Jesus is calling you. He does not simply want you to make it across into eternity. He cares for you way beyond that. Jesus wants you to spend eternity by His heart, not somewhere at a distance. He does not want to associate with you simply; Jesus wants to marry you.

Don't harden yourself as you read this book. If you know your heart is right in certain areas I am writing about, praise Him, and pray for your church and the church globally. If something I write irritates you, just pause and pray, "Holy Spirit, do Your thing in me!" Then, keep on reading.

I am sure you will be blessed and encouraged even though the message aims to challenge you.

Maranatha! Come, Lord Jesus, come!

ANTICIPATING JESUS

CHAPTER 1

THE END BEGINS WITH FAITH

JESUS IS COMING SOON. His coming is imminent. It can happen at any moment. The end-time cry is real. Jesus is coming for His Bride. The wedding date is set, and the Bride can feel it. She begins to ready herself.

It is vital to understand the importance of end-times to be the church that is ready to meet Jesus as the Bride. So, let's take it to the beginning of the end-time message. It is not in the book of Revelation. The critical word is encoded in the very definition of faith.

Without realizing it, when we accept Jesus in our hearts, we take on faith, which is end-time focused. Believing that Jesus Christ is the Savior is faith, but partial. The complete faith states that Jesus Christ is the Savior who died, rose, ascended, and is coming back again. The last part is often overlooked.

True faith cannot be separated from eschatology. Accelerated, multiplied, and purpose-driven faith is propelled by an expectancy of the second coming. This faith, which is seasoned with an end-time urgency, can save the modern church from complacency, religion, and deceit.

Every believer must always expect the imminent coming of the Messiah to keep a healthy spiritual life. I propose there is no alternative to acquiring faith that is pleasing to God. It is the only one. Let me make the case.

> **The end-time message is encoded in the very definition of faith**

"But without faith it is impossible to please Him" (Hebrews 11:6, KJV).

What is this faith that God responds to so well? I realize there are levels, and they cannot be equal. Only one can be pleasing to the Father.

There is faith that one could call demonic. Demons believe in God and tremble before Him (James 2:19), yet I do not think it is faith that God cares much about.

There is also an unbelieving faith. Many millions of people believe that God exists, but they do not live by the ways of God. They do not have fear or reverence for Him. This kind of faith is totally useless. It does not inspire the believer to take any action towards God. Can this faith be pleasing to God? I don't think so.

What kind of faith is pleasing to the Father? What kind of faith brings pleasure to His heart? It seems that the answer is not as apparent as one might think.

"But without faith it is impossible to please Him, for he who comes to God must believe that He is, and that He is a rewarder of those who diligently seek Him" (Hebrews 11:6, NKJV).

In this key verse, we can see that this faith has action. It is not static. This faith causes one to go on a journey. This faith is looking for something lost, and it is impossible to find it without diligence.

The heroes mentioned in the famous chapter eleven of Hebrews had that end-time faith that made them ready people walking in that pleasing faith. There is a pattern we can catch.

All those men were unique, with different gifts, talents, and historic achievements. Yet, on a foundational level, they were all remarkably the same.

"Now faith is the assurance of things hoped for, the conviction of things not seen. For by it the elders obtained a good testimony" (Hebrews 11:1–2, NKJV).

So, the elders of long ago have obtained a good testimony on behalf of God for their assurance in something they could not see. What were they so convinced of? What were they waiting for in hope? What unseen thing have they grabbed a hold of? What are we talking about here? We are making steps towards the foundational truth here. It will help you to become the Bride of Jesus.

Whenever we talk about faith that is pleasing to God, we have to ask ourselves what is actually pleasing to God. The answer is short—Jesus. Throughout the ages, God the Father responded only to one thing—His Son.

This is why we read about altars built by Abraham, Isaac, Jacob, Moses, and others. Whenever the altar would not be built, there would be no favor. But when someone built an altar, it pleased God, and success would follow.

This was because the altar is a picture of Jesus and His mission to be accomplished on the earth.

We can also see it in the blood sacrifices that people brought. They were received because they represented Jesus.

The law was good because it pointed to Jesus. God deliberately gave the law as a foreshadowing to His Son. The law was an Old Testament portrait of Jesus. The entire temple of Solomon was a picture of Jesus and what He was destined for.

In other words, God cannot accept or be pleased with anything outside of Jesus. The Father loves His Son so much that He will not recognize anything else. Anything outside of the Son is foreign. "Just as

He chose us in Him before the foundation of the world, that we should be holy and without blame before Him in love" (Ephesians 1:4, NKJV).

The only reason we, as Christians, are accepted by the Father is because of being in Christ. In other words, God accepts Jesus in whom we are hidden. We have nothing that may be pleasing or acceptable to God on our own.

"To the praise of His glorious grace and favor, which He so freely bestowed on us in the Beloved [His Son, Jesus Christ]" (Ephesians 1:6, AMP).

"And all these, having obtained a good testimony through faith, did not receive the promise, God having provided something better for us, that they should not be made perfect apart from us" (Hebrews 11:39–40, NKJV).

True faith is not rooted in striving but in stature.

We are reading here about some sort of perfection. A perfection that God the Father did not want the heroes of the Old Testament to obtain apart from us. They had to wait for us here in the New Testament era. There's only one perfection, and that is something we can attain in the one and only—in Jesus Christ.

Now, we are all in this together. The men of old and the men of new. Our faith can also be pleasing to God. This faith is not rooted in the striving but in stature. This faith is not about doing but in being.

The faith that is pleasing to God is the faith that is rooted in Christ. Digging deeper, I realized this is only half of the truth.

THE DIRECTION OF TRUE FAITH

There is much more to faith in Hebrews 11. The faith Paul highlights speaks of action, movement, and a specific direction. It was not some static faith of simply believing.

Every hero in that famous chapter was chasing something. Their faith caused them to do outrageous things and accomplish the impossible. They were motivated by something very real and definite.

That very thing is the Messiah. The men in chapter eleven not only knew about Him but also about His plan of redemption and wanted in on it. This makes faith that is truly pleasing to God a faith that believes in Jesus Christ and, critically important, anticipates His coming.

Paul claimed that the heroes of faith have all seen Jesus, physically or not, and their heroism was motivated solely by what He conveyed to them. Paul insisted that this was the sole reason for all the selfless courage we read about throughout the Old Testament.

These heroes of faith had a special relationship with Jesus. They saw Him centuries and even millenniums before He came down to this earth in a human body. This is pretty wild.

There is no way to avoid the fact that every hero mentioned greatly desired to see the coming of the Lord, and this is what stirred them to achieve the miraculous.

The apostle Paul understood this secret and conveyed it to the first church. Paul wanted to encourage the believers to do the same. He wrote, inspiring the early believers to live by a faith that expects the Lord's second coming. This is how Paul sought to prepare the church as the Bride.

Those heroes died and became a cloud of witnesses cheering the church on (Hebrews 12:1). They said, "You can do it. You can do the impossible and live supernaturally. Be courageous in the face of persecution. You can do it for the sake of Christ. He's coming soon. Don't give up. Just hold on a little longer."

I believe the expectancy of Jesus' return is the most significant missing piece in the modern church. This is also the biggest cause of the fallout that the church is experiencing.

No other vision can keep the modern church aligned, focused, and determined than the faith in the soon-coming Jesus Christ, who wants to marry her.

What would the Christian faith look like, realizing that Jesus is coming soon? What would our daily walk with God be like, knowing we must always be ready? If we can take this message seriously, our Christianity will be transformed into a radical and selfless movement. We will be fearless and focused to bring the Day of the Lord closer.

Every single New Testament author wrote about the second coming of Jesus. Pretty much every book of the New Testament contains a message about the great Day of the Lord and how it should motivate our daily lives.

The end-time message was never an afterthought or a once-a-year sermon. It was the driver of the first church. The very first sermon of the first church was based on this.

"Men of Galilee, why do you stand looking into heaven? This Jesus, who was taken up from you into heaven, will come in the same way as you saw him go into heaven" (Acts 1:11, ESV).

I believe this is the only way to bring the modern church back to the level of effectiveness that the first church had. To be consumed by one desire—the coming of Jesus, the Anointed One.

"Therefore, preparing your minds for action, and being sober-minded, set your hope fully on the grace that will be brought to you at the revelation of Jesus Christ" (1 Peter 1:13, ESV).

Let's take a deep dive to study the heroes of faith. Let's visit the places where they met the Messiah in the Old Testament, who promised His coming.

CHAPTER 2

OLD TESTAMENT JESUS

WHEN JESUS WAS BORN to the virgin Mary, it wasn't His first visit to Earth. It was His first time being born into a human body, but He came down to meet with people many times before.

Jesus is very social. He loves people and has difficulty restraining Himself from showing up. Jesus came often and was always very engaging.

Most of the visitations were not in a dream or a vision. They were not some ethereal angelic visitations. It was literally Jesus who showed up physically. He had real conversations, ate real human food, and had real interactions. People saw His face and lived.

Through these beautiful encounters with Jesus, people learned about His plan of salvation. Jesus revealed the future to them. Those encounters were revolutionary and shifted people to live by faith.

The revelation of His coming elevated the people to live supernatural lives. They did the impossible. Knowing the Messiah would surely come, they dared to risk everything for the life of victory. All earthly values paled. They wanted to be a part of the story. This is what the modern church desperately needs today.

EVE ANTICIPATED JESUS

When Adam and Eve sinned, it broke God's heart. He had to do what He did not want to. The Father had to punish the sin, sending Adam and Eve out of the garden. It was never His desire, but He had to do it.

God is not a man. He raises His kids differently than us. When we get disappointed with our kids sometimes, the natural response is, "Go away. I don't want to talk to you right now." When God is disappointed, He speaks promises and hopes. He never wants to turn anybody away and lead them into hopelessness.

Our God does not like dead ends and will never lead you to one. Some people prophecy, "God will punish you for this and that. Amen." If the prophetic word does not contain hope and a way out, it is likely not God.

The revelation of His coming elevated the people to live supernatural lives.

And so, even in the midst of this heavy distress, the Father gave Adam and Eve hope through a beautiful promise. He foretold that there would come a day when, through them, a Son would be born to make everything right again and reverse the curse by defeating the enemy.

"And I will put enmity between you and the woman, And between your seed and her Seed; He shall bruise your head, And you shall bruise His heel" (Genesis 3:15, NKJV). Adam and Eve have felt the dire difference living outside the garden of the Lord. Nothing came easy, and nothing was simple anymore. The anticipation for the promise of God seemed to be the only hope for a change.

Eve believed this word from the Lord and expected the Messiah to come. She wanted to reverse her mistake, which had swirled the entire world system into mayhem.

After some time, Eve got pregnant and gave birth to her firstborn son. She named him Cain, meaning "a man from the Lord" (Genesis 4:1). Cain was Eve's seed. She thought this was it. Here's the seed God spoke about. She probably thought, *Finally, we can return to the garden. This boy will make everything right.* Eve did not fully understand how terrible her sin was. She was almost naive.

The plan of God for Adam and Eve was to give birth to sons and daughters in the image of God. But after the fall, they could only bear sons and daughters in the image of Adam.

> **Flesh cannot give birth to Spirit, and Spirit cannot give birth to flesh.**

It did not take long for Eve to realize that Cain was not even close to the seed God mentioned. This caused great discouragement. Cain was anything but good. Even though the meaning of his name was great, he fell vastly short of that.

When Eve bore her second son, she named him Abel (Genesis 4:2). Abel was a good man, yet his name means "vanity" or "worthless." This speaks of how Eve got discouraged by Cain and did not believe her second son could be any better.

The growing realization of the vanity of life was unsettling. Eve was probably coming to the same conclusions as Ecclesiastes did. Everything was losing meaning.

Here is the truth that had to be learned. Jesus said in John 3:6 (ESV), "That which is born of the flesh is flesh, and that which is born of the Spirit is spirit." In other words, flesh cannot give birth to Spirit, and Spirit cannot give birth to flesh.

Interestingly enough, Adam faded into history and did not seem involved in these historical and deeply meaningful events (besides the fact that he'd get Eve pregnant).

Usually, it was the father who would give names to his children. It was supposed to be the father in the leadership role. But in this case, the Holy Spirit continues to uncover the story of humanity through Eve alone.

Some scholars suggest that Adam stopped bringing sacrifices to the Lord and may have completely abandoned faith. After all, being an image of the flesh, a complete contradiction to the second Adam—Jesus, there can only be one end. We will know what happened for sure in eternity.

After some time, Eve bore a third son and named him Seth (Genesis 4:25). His name means "the appointed substitution." This points us to the restoration of hope in Eve's life. I think she finally understood the truth and renewed her trust in the Lord.

Perhaps Seth was a picture of the spiritual birth John wrote about in John 1:13 (NKJV), "Who were born, not of blood, nor of the will of the flesh, nor of the will of man, but of God."

It was Seth with whom the lineage of Jesus began. The Messiah was destined to come through him. The beginning of Christ's genealogy through Seth stated the very destiny of Jesus.

By faith, Eve saw the unseen. She saw Jesus, the Seed (Galatians 3:16). At first, she tried to bring the day of salvation closer through her works and striving. But by the time she gave birth to Seth, she realized the true seed could only come by the Spirit.

Eve had a revelation of the seed, and she had a revelation that it would come at the right moment in history, specifically through Seth. Her faith was rooted in Christ and focused on the coming of the Messiah.

ABRAHAM ANTICIPATED JESUS

By faith Abraham, when he was tested, offered up Isaac, and he who had received the promises offered up his only begotten son, of whom it was said, "In Isaac your seed shall be called," concluding that God was able to raise him up, even from the dead, from which he also received him in a figurative sense.

Hebrews 11:17–19 (NKJV)

This verse supports the true faith with the fact that it includes the promise of the Messiah. Abraham had real faith, and it was founded on the promise of Jesus.

Abraham knew that Christ would come through his son Isaac. He was absolutely convinced beyond a shadow of a doubt. This is why Abraham boldly went up that mountain to sacrifice his son. He was confident that God would raise Isaac back from the dead. There was no other way because God's promises are always true.

Yes, because God made a promise, and the Word says faithful is the one that made a promise (Hebrews 10:23).

Abraham did not care about the details. He needed to know only one thing—God's word that the Messiah would come specifically through Isaac. This settled it.

But when did God tell Abraham about Jesus? We know He promised Abraham many children, but I don't recall a conversation about the One. At least I could not think of it quickly.

"Now to Abraham and his Seed were the promises made. He does not say, 'And to seeds,' as of many, but as of one, 'And to your Seed,' who is Christ" (Galatians 3:16, NKJV).

Amazing. We can see that God told Abraham about Christ, the Messiah, thousands of years before Jesus was born. It was a very specific conversation, not some vague exchange. It got Abraham excited. He wanted to see Him.

Not to mention the fact that Abraham met Jesus when He came with the other two angles on the way to Sodom and Gomorrah: "Then the men turned away from there and went toward Sodom, but Abraham still stood before the Lord" (Genesis 18:22, NKJV).

The word "Lord" in this verse is "Yahweh" in the original Hebrew. As James Maloney loved to say it, "Selah!"

MOSES ANTICIPATED JESUS

This gets even more interesting with the story of Moses.

> By faith Moses, when he became of age, refused to be called the son of Pharaoh's daughter, choosing rather to suffer affliction with the people of God than to enjoy the passing pleasures of sin, esteeming the reproach of Christ greater riches than the treasures in Egypt; for he looked to the reward.
> **Hebrews 11:24–26 (NKJV)**

Hold up. Hold up. The apostle Paul, I thought you were a prodigy and studied at the feet of Gamaliel. If you did, you probably were an F student. I'm just thinking to myself here.

Moses and Jesus are divided by about two thousand years. How can Paul write that Moses esteemed the reproach of Christ as anything? What kind of Christ are we talking about here? Jesus wasn't even close to being born yet, but Moses acted as though He was in the now, in the present. What?!

What if the Bible is still correct and it is not a contradiction? The apostle Paul knew exactly what he was writing.

Moses did see Jesus in front of him, even back in Egypt. This motivated him to make hard decisions. It gave him the strength to resist the biggest temptations of the time—the seduction of Egypt's most desired riches and power.

"By faith he forsook Egypt, not fearing the wrath of the king; for he endured as seeing Him who is invisible" (Hebrews 11:27, NKJV).

Moses did not see something invisible. Moses saw *someone* invisible. It was Jesus. This is what faith is all about—seeing the unseen. Not what is unseen, but who is unseen.

> **But faith is confident in the future because it is rooted in God's Word.**

Hope does not know what will happen in the future. It simply hopes. But faith has confidence in the future. It is rooted in the Word of God. Why? Because God is faithful to His Word. "For the word of the Lord is right and true; he is faithful in all he does" (Psalm 33:4, NIV).

Moses saw Jesus and understood His plan of salvation. This gave him such a boost of boldness and faith that he went on to be the greatest leader of Israel, bringing the Day of the Lord closer.

JACOB ANTICIPATED JESUS

Jacob saw Jesus and prophesied of His coming through Judah.

> The scepter shall not depart from Judah, Nor a lawgiver from between his feet, Until Shiloh comes; And to Him shall be the obedience of the people. Binding his donkey to the vine, And his donkey's colt to the choice vine, He washed his garments in wine, And his clothes in the blood of grapes. His eyes are darker than wine, And his teeth whiter than milk.
>
> **Genesis 49:10–12 (NKJV)**

Below are the notes taken from the commentaries of *The Passion Translation* of the book of Genesis.[2]

In this case, the name Shiloh is attributed to the Messiah. He came and took what was due to Him. When Jesus stood before Pilate, the people turned over the authority to rule to the foreigners (the Romans).

This was a sign that Shiloh, the One whose right it was to rule, had come. He took that staff of authority to rule over the nations.

It was his last match when Jacob met and wrestled with God in the wilderness. You have to admit Jacob was a stubborn wrestler. He struggled at his birth and lost. He also contended that night with God and lost.

In the root, the name Jacob means a wrestler. There is an amazing play on words in Hebrew between the words "he wrestled" (*ye'abeq*), "empty himself" (*yabboq*), and Jacob or "to supplant" (*yaaqob*).

Jacob had to lose, but nothing is better than losing to God. He had to lose his old identity to begin to represent Christ in the core of His being. When finally God blessed Jacob, He gave him a new name, "Israel," which means "prince with God."

Later down through the chapters, we can see that the Bible goes back and forth between the two names. This always puzzled me.

It means that the Holy Spirit would call him Jacob whenever Jacob acted according to the flesh. But the Holy Spirit would call him Israel whenever he acted according to the Spirit. All actions in the Spirit were the right moves toward the coming of Christ.

JOSEPH ANTICIPATED JESUS

Joseph was a big believer in the coming of the Messiah. For this reason, he did not want his bones to stay in Egypt and demanded they be taken together with the Israelites when they left. By faith, he knew it would indeed happen.

In the Bible, Joseph's life bears the closest resemblance to Jesus:

- Joseph was loved by Jacob. Jesus was loved by God.
- Joseph was in the pit. Jesus was in the grave.

- Joseph was sold for twenty coins. Jesus was slightly more expensive and went for thirty coins.
- Egypt was blessed for the sake of Joseph. We are blessed for the sake of Jesus.
- Joseph was tested in everything, just like Jesus was.
- Joseph forgave his brothers for their wrongdoings. Jesus forgave us for our wrongdoings.
- Joseph always glorified God just like Jesus glorified the Father.
- Joseph was humiliated and lifted high. Jesus' first coming was a humiliation. His second coming will be glorious.
- Jacob thought Joseph was dead, just like the disciples thought Jesus was dead.
- Joseph cried seeing his brothers not believing they were truly forgiven. Jesus cried seeing the unbelief of Israel.
- Joseph was thirty years of age when he entered the service of Pharaoh. Jesus was thirty when He began His earthly ministry.
- Joseph was given a bride by the Pharoh. Jesus will be given a Bride by the Father.

There is so much more depth in Joseph's life. I recommend a deep study on his life through the lens of Jesus Christ.

MANY OTHERS ANTICIPATED JESUS

There were many others who met the Messiah in the Old Testament. They understood the end-time message clearly and were driven by the ultimate awareness and desire to see the Day of the Lord come.

Abel saw Jesus by faith. He had brought a sheep sacrifice (blood sacrifice) to God from the finest of His flock. Abel understood the heart of God. It is interesting to note that before the flood, sheep were not used for food, only for sacrifice (Genesis 1:29). This is one of the reasons why his sacrifice was acceptable. It signified what Jesus would do many centuries later.

Enoch and God were intimate friends. This is why God revealed deep secrets of the future to him. Enoch was the seventh man from Adam. He was a prophet who foretold events as far as the second coming (Jude 1:14–15). He received a revelation about the return of Christ.

Enoch had a son named Methuselah, which means "when he dies, it will be sent" or "his death shall send." Enoch gave him a prophetic name because the year Methuselah died was the year the flood was sent. Enoch was aware of those future days, and it moved him.

There is also a profound reason why Methuselah was the longest-living person on the earth (he lived for 969 years). Pastor Alan DiDio draws a beautiful conclusion, saying that during those many years, Methuselah was a living warning of the imminent judgment, but because of God's mercy and long patience, He waited as long as he could, extending Methuselah's days.[3] He did not want the people to perish, but no one listened to the news of the end times.

Leading up to Noah, there are nine names in the line of Seth. Their meanings are: "man," "appointed," "mortality," "lament of death," splendor of God," "descends," "his death will bring," "powerful-overcoming," and "rest and comfort."

Putting these names together in one sentence, we uncover the hidden theme in the genealogy of Adam: "Man is appointed to mortality, and the lament of death, but the splendor of God (Jesus Christ) will descend, and his death will bring the powerful overthrow of death and sin to bring us rest and comfort."[4]

The promise of the coming Jesus was everywhere in the Old Testament. The people of faith got the memo, and they dreamed of that day to come.

> Then the Lord (Yahweh) appeared to him and said: "Do not go down to Egypt; live in the land of which I shall tell you...

> And I will make your descendants multiply as the stars of heaven; I will give to your descendants all these lands; and in your seed all the nations of the earth shall be blessed.
>
> **Genesis 26:2; 26:4 (NKJV)**[5]

Yahweh came to *Isaac* and told him about the seed to come in whom all the nations of the earth will be blessed. This could have only meant one thing—Jesus. No other blessing can cover the world like the Gospel of Jesus Christ.

Gideon saw Jesus face to face. The LORD turned to Gideon and said, "Go with your strength and save Israel from the Midianites. I am the one who is sending you" (Judges 6:14, NCV).

In Hebrew, the word "Lord" is "Yahweh." It was not an angel but God Himself who appeared to Gideon, turning a fearful man into a fearsome warrior. Just like the Holy Spirit converted the disciples into bold and victorious believers.

David anticipated Jesus. He wrote about the Messiah extensively and predicted His crucifixion in great detail. Psalm 22 even quotes the phrases Jesus would say over a thousand years later while on the cross.

Shadrach, *Meshach*, and *Abednego* were probably shocked to see a fourth man walking into the fire. Yep, that was Jesus. Nebuchadnezzar screamed in shock, "I see four men loose, walking in the midst of the fire; and they are not hurt, and the form of the fourth is like the Son of God" (Daniel 3:25, NKJV).

King Solomon had encounters with Jesus. He wrote prophetic poetry in the book of Proverbs. Many see that book as simply a cheat sheet for life. It is far more than that. This book is about Jesus uncovering who He was before the creation, what He will do on the earth, and how He will die for our sins. It's all in there.

"Come, eat of my bread And drink of the wine I have mixed. Forsake foolishness and live, And go in the way of understanding" (Proverbs 9:5–6, NKJV).

This is talking about the body and the blood of Jesus. "Jesus stood and cried out, saying, "If anyone thirsts, let him come to Me and drink. He who believes in Me, as the Scripture has said, out of his heart will flow rivers of living water" (John 7:37–38, NKJV).

I listed some of the encounters people had with Jesus in the Old Testament. The Bible doesn't mention everyone's story of those encounters, but the apostle Paul adds the names of Barak, Samson, Jephthah, and Samuel to the list.

JESUS PROVES THE POINT

Even Jesus Himself said in Luke 10:24 (NKJV), "For I tell you that many prophets and kings have desired to see what you see, and have not seen it, and to hear what you hear, and have not heard it."

The prophets and the kings of old knew Jesus. They understood how blessed the people would be to see Him one day. They had that holy envy for the generation that would see everything Jesus would do and hear everything He would teach. Somehow, they understood it clearly.

This verse states that the men of old knew the plan of salvation centuries before it happened. They knew exactly what it would be and through whom it would come. This is why they desired to see it.

The believers of the Old Testament strived to see Jesus. They longed for the One to come and make everything right. The one that will reconcile the people back to God. Being driven by this, the men of old lived heroic lifestyles. They wished for one thing only—the Messiah.

We have learned here that faith is not simply a belief in Jesus. True faith is a belief in Jesus, who is coming soon. The apostle Paul says it is this faith specifically that can help us live in victory.

"Therefore we also, since we are surrounded by so great a cloud of witnesses, let us lay aside every weight, and the sin which so easily ensnares us, and let us run with endurance the race that is set before us" (Hebrews 12:1, NKJV).

This is the faith that will ensure the Bride is ready. It is an endtime faith surrounded by those who have believed the same way in the past and were not disappointed. If you are expecting the coming of the Lord, you are not alone.

You may not be a majority here on earth, but you will not be outnumbered with the cloud of witnesses cheering you on from the heavens. The men of faith in the Old Testament showed an example for us. They showed us how to live by faith that eagerly waits for the One you love and the supernatural outcome of that.

John the Baptist, the last of the Old Testament prophets, said to his disciples,

> You've heard me tell you that I am not the Messiah, but certainly I am the messenger sent ahead of him. He is the Bridegroom, and the bride belongs to him. I am the friend of the Bridegroom who stands nearby and listens with great joy to the Bridegroom's voice. Because of his words, my joy is complete and overflows!
>
> **John 3:28–29 (TPT)**

The Bridegroom is coming back one last time. His first visit was an engagement. "Now He who has prepared us for this very thing is God, who also has given us the Spirit as a guarantee" (2 Corinthians 5:5, NKJV).

The Passion Translation puts it like this: "And to confirm this promise, he has given us the Holy Spirit, like an engagement ring, as a guarantee."

Now, He is returning to marry the Bride in a resolution of a dramatic and the most beautiful story we get to be a part of.

CHAPTER 3

THE FIRST CHURCH ANTICIPATED JESUS

MOVING ALONG THE HISTORY leading up to the birth of Jesus, we can feel how the anticipation of the Messiah grew stronger and stronger. It's been many centuries and millenniums. The four hundred years leading up to Jesus' birth passed in deafening silence—the calm before the storm.

The desperation to finally see the promised King culminated under the ruthless rulership of the Roman Empire. If not now, then when? Things are only getting worse.

On top of that, the prophecies of the past ages began to align. People started talking, and the rumors began to circulate. The chit-chatters about the Messiah who is to come soon spread like wildfire. Everyone could fill it in the air: the anticipation, the hopeful excitement. It was about to happen.

I can only imagine the cultural moment of that day. It was impossible to keep down the talks of the promised Savior. Everyone is adding up the times.

Herod knew it. The foreign wise men knew it. They came out of nowhere looking for the new King. The scribes reading through the scrolls determined His birth's location and correct timing. The Messiah must already be down here somewhere, walking among the people.

When the massacre of children took place in Bethlehem, everyone knew why. It was a day not quickly forgotten. We don't know much about the details, but it must have taken generations to get over it. What a tragedy.

Then there was this Hannah at the temple who probably could not stop talking about the baby she saw a few days ago. She recognized Him by the spirit.

Simeon, the priest, told everyone he would not die until he saw the Messiah. Then, one random day, he saw this baby and recognized the One. Simeon prayed over Him and declared that He was Christ indeed.

Some might have been skeptical until a few days later, when Simeon passed away. There are writings that state Simeon "uttered the benediction and died."[6] It is possible he passed away the same day.

There was so much breaking news all a few days apart. Everyone was on their tiptoes. "When Herod the king heard this, he was troubled, and all Jerusalem with him" (Matthew 2:3, ESV).

Yet, no one could identify the family of Jesus. So much noise and trouble one day, and the next all vanished.

A TEMPORARY RELIEF

So much expectation, and then silence for another thirty years. Where is He? What was the point of all the commotion?

Some people probably counted Messiah's approximate age based on everything that happened. I imagine people conversing, "He must be around thirteen by now"; "He should be about twenty-five or so"; "Based on everything that happened, Christ is probably around thirty now"; "I wonder if He will reveal Himself shortly. If He ever will, it's about time. We need freedom now"; "These Romans have no idea what is coming at them."

Then, Jesus finally revealed His identity. The Father and the Holy Spirit confirmed it at His baptism. Jesus, the only Son of God, the One the Earth had been groaning for through the millenniums, is now walking among the mortals. It was a fantastic time to see the Son of God in person, hear Him utter the most profound truths, and see Him perform the most astounding miracles.

It all was true. The long-awaited Messiah had come. Everything added up. Everything made sense. This was like a fairy tale—the Son of God living among men. It was heaven on earth. If only it could stay this way forever.

The people probably thought Jesus would walk around for some time through the cities and then get to the real business—the overthrowing of the Roman Empire. But Jesus did not extend His time on earth. Only three and a half years of the actual ministry as the Savior. That was it. And the Messiah was gone. Died, arose, and gone again.

People waited for the Messiah for thousands of years. He came and went so quickly. So greatly anticipated and desired, yet missing once more.

Every author of the New Testament wrote about the second coming of Jesus.

After this brief relief, the men of faith returned to this mode of anticipation. They went back to waiting again. But now they are not waiting for Christ's coming. They are waiting for His return—the second coming.

EARLY BELIEVERS ANTICIPATED JESUS

The first church did not steer away from the same vision of the Old Testament heroes. They longed to see Jesus again and took on this mission of expectancy. Jesus had to leave so that His Bride could get ready.

As I mentioned earlier, every author of the New Testament wrote about the second coming of Jesus and how it should move us to live pure and righteous lives. This inspired the church to live supernatural lifestyles similar to the heroes of faith in the Old Testament.

For example, the apostle Paul was beaten to death. The Holy Spirit resurrected him. He got up and went back to do what got him killed in the first place. One could say, "You've done enough, Paul. You have fought until the shedding of your blood. You're excused now." Why did Paul keep going?

The unstoppable desire to keep spreading the Gospel at the risk of losing his life was because Paul saw someone before him. He saw someone by faith—Jesus, whose arrival he wanted to bring closer.

"And let us consider one another in order to stir up love and good works, not forsaking the assembling of ourselves together, as is the manner of some, but exhorting one another, and so much the more as you see the Day approaching" (Hebrews 10:24–25, NKJV).

Let's not point fingers at those who attend church only once a month, but Paul's point is serious. There is a reason why he encouraged the believers always to be together and do good works in love.

Do good things. Be loving. Don't neglect the church gatherings. What is the primary motivation for all of this, if you ask Paul? Because the Day of the Lord is approaching quickly. This is what drove the early believers.

Today, we attend church for great music, coffee, and a dynamic speaker. While all these things are fantastic, what should move us is the fact that Jesus is about to return.

Even our ancestors, parents, grandparents, and those who lived through the Soviet Union were the heroes of faith. They longed for Jesus. This is what motivated them to stay faithful under heavy persecution.

It was not a human stubbornness. When they were sent off to Syberia and stripped of opportunities, they saw Jesus before them all those years. They did not want to make any decision that would hinder their dream— to be a ready Bride for Christ.

"So Christ was offered once to bear the sins of many. To those who eagerly wait for Him He will appear a second time, apart from sin, for salvation" (Hebrews 9:28, NKJV).

Some theologians like Irving Baxter suggested that five of the seven trumpets have already sounded.[7] I know some internationally recognized pastors and preachers who are convinced that Jesus will return during their lifetime. Some of them are over sixty years old. This means they believe Jesus will return within twenty or thirty years.

I am not saying these theologians are one hundred percent correct, but some credible people who have been studying the Bible all their lives do believe that.

"For I have betrothed you to one husband, that I may present you as a chaste virgin to Christ" (2 Corinthians 11:2, NKJV).

The first church had a clear objective: to become a pure bride. This was the driving force behind their generosity, commitment, bravery, and selflessness. This is what drove them to get together, to fast, to pray, and to intercede for one another. They did whatever it took to make sure they were ready as the Bride, and whenever the first church fell short, just like it happened in the Old Testament, God used people like the apostles and the prophets to straighten them out.

With the biblical example of the heroes from the Old and the New Testaments, we can see clearly that the end-time message must be foundational for every believer and church. It is to be the passion of our being. This is the biblical lifestyle to live out.

Only the end-time call can prepare the Bride, while everything else leads to complacency. But who is this Bride? As Solomon wrote, "Who is this coming up from the wilderness, Leaning upon her beloved?" (Song of Solomon 8:5, NKJV). How can I be ready as the Bride? Is every believer a Bride automatically? Let's meet this Bride of Christ.

CHAPTER 4

THE BRIDE ANTICIPATES JESUS

MEET THE BRIDE

I WANT TO BREAK DOWN THE LAST CHAPTER of the book of Proverbs to paint a picture of a believer Jesus is looking to marry. Proverbs 31 is the portrait of the true Bride. We can see all her beauty in that incredible poem.

Chapter thirty-one was written by King Lemuel. He wrote the words that his mother taught him. It is believed that Lemuel is a pseudonym for Solomon. This would make Bathsheba give these words of wisdom to her son.

Bathsheba began by telling her son to stay pure and away from a wayward woman. She also wrote that it is not suitable for a king to drink alcohol. She went further and commanded her son not to crave it (Proverbs 31:4). It was inappropriate for his stature. Allow me to remind all believers that we are kings and priests in God's kingdom (Revelation 5:10).

Starting in verse 10 and continuing to the end of the book, Lemuel writes his mother's words about a radiant bride. The entire book of Proverbs is written as poetry, but these last words are written in a totally unique style.

Proverbs 31:10–31 is communicated alphabetically in structure, with each of the twenty-two verses beginning with a consecutive letter of the Hebrew alphabet.[8] This style implies that a godly wife is a woman who exhausts the entire language. She is so magnificent and beautiful that it takes the entire language to describe her. She is a perfect bride.

I don't know about you, but the last chapter of Proverbs makes me feel like this describes an ideal wife who makes her husband look like the luckiest and the laziest man alive.

I can see how this poem can relate to a wife, but can any woman attain such a high standard?! It is humanly impossible. Wives are already too hard on themselves. They already carry so much on their shoulders: home, food, kids, school, some even carry their husbands, etc.

> **The Bride is so magnificent it takes an entire language to describe her.**

The poem says this woman never sleeps, cares for everyone, cooks, does business, helps the poor, and gets the family dressed. Guess what her husband is doing. He's sitting at the gates of the city. Man, I want to be him.

This describes many modern husbands. I have a friend whose sixty-year-old dad still plays video games. He must have a very good wife to be able to do that and not go hungry.

I once told my wife that no one is perfect and she should embrace her mistakes. She agreed, came up to me, and hugged me. Smile if you can.

Honestly, though, my wife came very close to this perfect wife. When I was awfully sick for over four years, she carried me and all the household burdens by herself. I had chronic issues with my back, and for the most part, I could only sit or lie down.

I had back issues all my life, but they escalated and caused me to be, as the doctor put it, "an inch from being disabled." Thankfully, by the stripes of Jesus, I got supernaturally healed.

Before the miracle, my wife cared for all our four kids. It was especially difficult at night as our babies were terrible sleepers. With our fourth baby, Natalie hadn't slept one whole night in over a year, and I could not help in any way because of the excruciating pain I would go through waking up at night.

Even today, I could never do what I do without her. After eleven years together, I can now say that I would never be who I am without her. Many of my revelations come through our conversations about God and the Scriptures. We kick off each other well because she is full of wisdom and uncompromising love for the Word (but I digress).

While some teach that Proverbs 31 is about a godly wife, others go further to show how this chapter is about the church. I propose that this chapter defines the Bride of Christ. Jesus is the bridegroom, and this radiant woman in the poem is His Bride.

You may ask, "Well, what is the difference between the church and the Bride? Aren't they the same thing? Does that mean you can make it to heaven and not be the Bride?"

What I am about to write to you is one of the most resisted messages by the religious spirit. The devil hates it. Don't believe it? Try preaching it. Feel free to share it at your church and see what happens.

> **Not all church is the Bride of Christ.**

I recall the testimony of my grandfather, Adam Gritskevich. He was caught up in heaven many times. His body would lay dead for over nine hours while he would spend time in heaven. He would come back perfectly healthy and share the stories of his encounters.

My grandfather was a pastor and a prophet. One thing he always told his church and especially his family was, "Being saved is marvelous. But, my children, strive to be a part of His Bride. The glory is incomparable."

My grandfather was persecuted for this by the religious leaders. They were enraged, saying how dare he teach that not all church is the Bride of Christ. All the while, the Bible makes a clear distinction.

His daughter, my mom, keeps this fire going, telling us—her nine kids—to continuously pursue a closer relationship with Jesus to be in the Bride.

The Bride is a special group of people within the church. I want to uncover this to challenge you and cast a greater vision for your life. People become Christians by walking through the door that is Jesus Christ. So often, they get saved and walk around wondering and lost, not knowing what's next.

Is there anything else besides the Sunday service? Do I just read the Bible and behave? Where do I go from here? There is a greater purpose. There is more to being saved than avoiding the lake of fire. God is calling us into an intimate relationship—to become His Bride.

THE PICTURE OF THE BRIDE

Let's read this poem together in a new light. Many comments below are taken from the commentaries in *The Passion Translation*. Proverbs 31:10–31 (NKJV):

10. "Who can find a virtuous wife? For her worth is far above rubies."

Virtuous in Hebrew is *khayil*. It is often used in connection with military prowess. It translates as mighty, wealthy, excellent, and morally upright. This is a warring wife. Her worth is priceless because she was paid by the blood of the Lamb, her Bridegroom.

11. "The heart of her husband safely trusts her; So he will have no lack of gain."

Her Bridegroom has great confidence in her. There is no jealousy or suspicion.

12. "She does him good and not evil all the days of her life."

She brings honor to Him and not disgrace. Jesus is not ashamed of her. Her faithfulness is consistent, not seasonal.

13. "She seeks wool and flax, And willingly works with her hands."

Wool is a metaphor for purity. Linen speaks of righteousness. The priests used to wear linen garments. The curtains of the tabernacle were made of linen. The Bride of Christ seeks what is only pure and righteous.

The hands represent the five ministries of Jesus: apostles, prophets, evangelists, pastors, and teachers. She delights in equipping others.

14. "She is like the merchant ships, She brings her food from afar."

The Bride brings spiritual food from the depths of the Spirit, like the manna from heaven. Jesus was described as a merchant in Matthew 13:45, who gave everything to purchase the "pearl," which is a believer.

15. "She also rises while it is yet night, And provides food for her household, and a portion for her maidservants."

She is interceding through the night for others. The Bride of Jesus will arise to feed the people of God. Maidservants represent other churches and ministries.

16. "She considers a field and buys it; From her profits she plants a vineyard."

Buying a field reflects on the parable of Jesus recorded in Matthew 13:44–46. The vineyard is a metaphor for the local church. We are the branches of the Vine (Jesus).

17. "She girds herself with strength, And strengthens her arms."

She is anointed with power from the Holy Spirit.

18. "She perceives that her merchandise is good, And her lamp does not go out by night."

Her work for the Lord is pleasing. She is consistent and true even in dark seasons. The lamp represents the prayer life. She overcomes even in the culture of darkness.

19. "She stretches out her hands to the distaff, And her hand holds the spindle."

She is prosperous and generous to help the needy. She wears clothes of righteousness (Colossians 3:12).

20. "She extends her hand to the poor, Yes, she reaches out her hands to the needy."

Her hands are mentioned a lot in this poem, highlighting yet again the ministry of Jesus through the church.

21. "She is not afraid of snow for her household, For all her household is clothed with scarlet."

Snow can represent tribulations. Scarlet clothes represent blood. The blood of Jesus covers her family.

22. "She makes tapestry for herself; Her clothing is fine linen and purple."

This speaks of the body of Christ that is united, woven, and knit together.

23. "Her husband is known in the gates, When he sits among the elders of the land."

This is the place of judgment as it was done in those days. Her Bridegroom is a judge.

24. "She makes linen garments and sells them, And supplies sashes for the merchants."

Again, highlighting her works of righteousness. She is a capable woman.

25. "Strength and honor are her clothing; She shall rejoice in time to come."

Or "she laughs at the days to come." She has no fear of the future. She is eternity-driven because she will be married to her Bridegroom.

26. "She opens her mouth with wisdom, And on her tongue is the law of kindness."

She is merciful and without compromise. She knows the ways of the Lord.

27. "She watches over the ways of her household, And does not eat the bread of idleness."

She is the watchman over her house. She does not conform to the culture and does not waste her time on vanity.

28. "Her children rise up and call her blessed; Her husband also, and he praises her:"

She is not a barren woman. The true church of Christ grows in salvations, and the believers grow spiritually to love Jesus. To see how her husband praises her, read *Songs of Songs*.

29. "Many daughters have done well, But you excel them all."

Previous generations of true believers did well, but the church of the last days will be incomparably more glorious.

30. "Charm is deceitful and beauty is passing, But a woman who fears the Lord, she shall be praised."

She is not focused on the external, fleshly desires. She is totally consumed and devoted to the love of God.

31. "Give her of the fruit of her hands, And let her own works praise her in the gates."

She will be rewarded because of her character based on the fruit of the Spirit. She will be honored at the wedding feast that is quickly approaching. She will be rewarded according to her works.

NOT EVERY BELIEVER IS THE BRIDE

This is a complete description of the Bride of Christ. Do you realize that not all believers and churches fit this picture? To live as the Bride is a commitment on an entirely different level.

Christianity that shows up to church twice a year does not fit this profile. The average Sunday Christian does not fit the Bride's description. Simply repeating the salvation prayer won't do it. Opening a Bible on a rare occasion and praying ten minutes a week is not a characteristic of the Bride in love.

> **Being the Bride is a commitment on a whole different level**

This is about a believer whose love and devotion to Jesus is without reserve.

The Bride of Christ is the number one interest of Jesus, and the Bride's responsibility is to get ready. The brides today go through many ceremonies to prepare themselves. They do test rounds of makeup and hair. On their wedding day, they pretty much do not sleep. Their friends start preparing them at four in the morning. They don't even eat. Dare the belly show.

When the bride gets ready, no one will allow the bridegroom to enter the house until she is ready to shine. You will not find a culture on this earth where the bridegroom prepares the bride. He cannot even see her until she is ready. So, you and I have work to do. We need to be ready to present ourselves before Jesus.

It is just like Esther, who could not enter before the king as the bride until she got ready. It took her a bit of time. For the first six months, she prepared with oil of myrrh and the second six months with perfumes for the purpose of beautifying herself (Esther 2).

Nowadays, when we want to enter the Holy of Holies into the presence of the King of Kings, we pray, "Just take me as I am!" Don't get it mistaken. The first time you come to God, you can come as you are, but you cannot stay as you are.

Your first spiritual bath is to wash off the stinky stuff. Don't stop there. You can also bathe in the Word and the presence to beautify yourself and be Bride-worthy.

"...Just as Christ also loved the church and gave Himself for her, that He might sanctify and cleanse her with the washing of water by the word" (Ephesians 5:25–26, NKJV).

The church is anyone who accepts Jesus as their Lord and Savior. Everyone who sincerely believes and professes Jesus as their Lord becomes a part of the church. But the Bride has a different relationship and a different dedication.

You can come as you are, but you cannot stay as you are

She is not only taking the righteousness of Christ, but she is also giving something in return. You will be saved even though you may be a self-centered person. You can take all the goodies from Jesus: forgiveness, righteousness, holiness. You may live by the flesh and, who knows, maybe still make it to heaven. The Bride, though, is different.

Some guys get cringy with this analogy, "How do you marry Jesus? He is a man, and I am a man. It is easier for the girls to understand it." One of my friends said, "We even sing too many girly songs at church. They're all about love, kisses, embraces."

I know this doesn't make sense in the natural, but I feel so good that it gives butterflies in my stomach thinking about His love. I don't mind if this analogy is feminine and calls me a bride. The Holy Spirit is okay with it, so I will not be offended. I am soaking in His love.

Look, when Enoch walked with God, and God took him to Himself, the original meaning of the phrase "God took him" is the Hebrew word *laqach*, which can also mean "God took him in marriage," just like a man takes a bride in marriage. This is beautiful.

Lord, take me in marriage like you took Enoch. I want to walk that intimately with You.

God gave a bride out of Adam's side. Jesus was stabbed in the side so we could become His Bride (John 19:34). We can if only we are willing to stay at His side. Just like John, who often reclined at the chest of Jesus, soaking in the love (John 13:23). He was not offended but proud that he could rest in the arms of Jesus. He boasted about it repeatedly.

In the *Ladies of Gold* (Volume 3) book, James Maloney writes from the journals of the praying ladies who dedicated themselves to intercede every night for over fifty years, "On her Coronation Day it will be surprising to discover that in this select company are some of the lowliest and most obscure of saints-hidden ones who were unknown and unsung among men, but well known to heaven and the King!"[9]

I WANT TO GET MARRIED

Jesus will sit on His throne, and beside Him will be the Queen, that Bride that is now married. I can only imagine what will happen next.

The thought of eternity amazes me. The Bible says that God makes everything new, and I can only fantasize what this marriage union will create. Maybe new life or new worlds or new frontiers. It is unimaginable and unexplainable right now.

As the Queen of the King, I believe she will be doing those new things together with Jesus. Eternity is so much greater than avoiding hell or making it to heaven.

Let's get down to earth here because we have to admit that not every believer fits the description you have been reading about. Not every Christian lives this lifestyle. This is why I want to challenge you to go for more, go higher, read further.

The Lord promised the Laodiceans, "To him that overcometh will I grant to sit with me in my throne, even as I also overcame, and am set down with my Father in his throne" (Revelation 3:21, KJV).

The Bride of Christ is not hard to find in the crowd. She stands out by her victorious way of living. She is an overcomer. She walks in the light, in the spirit. She is without bitterness or defeat. She lives in the union with the will of God even when the people despise her and hate her.

I want to be worthy of this calling. This is my life's goal. If being the Bride requires living a simpler life, so be it. I will do it if it means I need to be more generous. If I need to forgive, I will. If I need to move to do something radical in obedience, sign me up.

Every bitterness and offense can be justified but will not benefit you in eternity.

I am not going to man-please anyone. Many people want to be approved by the crowd, which affects how they preach or do any other ministry. But I have only one person I want to please—the Bridegroom. This is my desire.

Let me ask you. What are the acts of righteousness that Jesus wants you to do? What acts of unrighteousness do you need to stop doing right now?

It is time to leave jealousy behind. It is okay if your neighbor is doing better than you. It is okay if his house is bigger and his car is fancier. It is not about that for you.

When people hurt you, you forgive them. You choose to live an unoffendable life. Every bitterness and offense can be justified but will not benefit you in eternity. Get rid of it, for your sake.

"For the marriage of the Lamb has come, and His wife has made herself ready" (Revelation 19:7, NKJV).

This is an amazing promise. There will be a time when the remnant of the church will become ready. It will not be easy because this is who the enemy hates the most. But they will be people who eagerly await the revealing of the Son while fulfilling the great commandment through the acts of righteousness.

"And the dragon was enraged with the woman, and he went to make war with the rest of her offspring, who keep the commandments of God and have the testimony of Jesus Christ" (Revelation 12:17, NKJV).

The remnant is rising, and I want to be one of them. With the help of the Holy Spirit, I want to live a Proverbs 31 lifestyle.

Based on that beautiful poem, I want Jesus to entrust me with His reputation. I never want to be ashamed of Him. Instead, I want to be vocal about Him.

I remember while in college, I was telling my classmates about my missionary trips. I shared how I saw crazy healings of crippled standing up and blind eyes opening. All my peers just stared at me. It was all too unusual to hear.

In the evening, I got an email from one of my classmates. She wrote that it was so awesome for me to share Jesus boldly. She added, "I am a Christian too." I was surprised.

Like what?! It had been almost two years, and I never knew she was a believer. And the only way she felt bold enough to reveal it was via email.

The Bride of Christ is noticeable. Everyone will quickly figure her out at work, college, or school.

I want to proclaim His name like the Bride does in the poem. I want to be pure and righteous like she is described. I want to be diligent and bear fruit. I want to be known as the man of prayer interceding for others.

It is one thing to enjoy His presence in prayer. It is another thing to fight on behalf of others in intercession. Are there people in your life that you are fighting for in your prayer life?

I want to be bold and never live in fear, joyfully looking into the future.

Many are filled with anxiety when they consider the days ahead. A deacon came up to do the offering message at a church I visited. He started to cry, sharing how things were so bad. The economy caused his business to struggle. He was losing money. All his friends were panicking. The recession was so bad. And then he called the ushers to collect the tithes and offerings.

This was probably the worst church offering message I have ever heard of. I can only imagine the amount collected on that particular Sunday.

When you are the Bride of Christ, you laugh at the future. You don't live in fear. You live in faith. It is not easy. It is never a one-time lesson you pass, causing you to always be in faith. But it is possible if you are alert.

I want God to do mighty exploits and miracles through me for His glory, just like in the poem.

I hope you can see that not the entire church or all the believers fit the Bride's profile. It suits a remnant of people who live a particular spiritually elevated lifestyle. I hope you can see it and get excited about becoming one if you are not. Today is the call for you and me to rise up.

> There are sixty queens And eighty concubines, And virgins without number. My dove, my perfect one, Is the only one, The only one of her mother, The favorite of the one who bore her. The daughters saw her And called her blessed, The queens and the concubines, And they praised her.
>
> **Song of Solomon 6:8–9 (NKJV)**

This verse shows us varying degrees of dedication to Jesus. They are different union levels with Him. All are privileged, but only one is highlighted as the favorite, so much so that all other degrees of union praise her. She is not one of the queens. She is the Queen.

This is the company I want to be in. I pray the Lord renews us to get excited and actively pursue it. Will you take the challenge to live by different standards? Will you decide to be more than just a churchgoer with good morals today? Will you pursue Jesus until He is the One and Only desire of your heart? Let's do it together with a company of people who will not be satisfied until they are unified with the Bridegroom.

> God himself is the one who has prepared us for this wonderful destiny. And to confirm this promise, he has given us the Holy Spirit, like an engagement ring, as a guarantee. That's why we're always full of courage. Even while we're at home in the body, we're homesick to be with the Master.
>
> **2 Corinthians 5:5–6 (TPT)**

The Bridegroom loves you and wants you. Say "yes" to His proposal. You will never live to regret it. Say "yes" just like the men of faith did, just like the first church did. Though you may struggle in the flesh until He comes, you will have all the strength and courage to overcome temptations and attacks. You will be ready and worthy of the high calling of the Bride of Christ.

CHAPTER 5

DOES THE MODERN CHURCH ANTICIPATE JESUS?

SKIPPING WITH JESUS

JUST LIKE JESUS USED TO COME PHYSICALLY down to earth in the Old Testament, He still does that today. Nothing forbids Him to do so. We can easily find countless testimonies of people encountering the physical presence of Jesus. This is now especially common in Muslim countries.

My grandfather, Adam Gritskevich, was a pastor and a prophet in Belarus. He served as a pastor in the eighties until his death in 1992. Belarus was a communist country that heavily persecuted Christians. Bibles were scarce. Any religious literature was forbidden.

During those difficult years, Jesus would personally visit my grandfather. Adam used to wake up with the sunrise and go into the fields to mow the grass for the cattle. Jesus used to often appear to him in a physical form and spend hours conversing, teaching my grandfather everything church-related.

Adam would later walk with his kids, my mom was one of them, through those places and tell them, "This place is holy. This rock right here is where Jesus sat." Whenever I visit the village where I grew up, Dubitsa, I go to those places and try to imagine how it may have been. How was it to meet Jesus personally, physically on earth?!

When I was seven years old, in 1996, I got the same opportunity to meet Jesus face to face. My mom, Anna, was pregnant with a baby girl, but a night before labor, she had terrible internal bleeding caused by the reckless actions of her doctor. The baby girl died, as well as my mom.

This news broke us all. I remember many relatives, uncles, and aunts at our house crying and weeping uncontrollably over what had happened.

As everyone travailed, I went upstairs to my bed, dropped on my knees, and prayed as a seven-year-old could. I prayed for the Lord to save my mom. I missed her so much that I remember that feeling even now. She hasn't been home in a while. I could not picture the thought of never seeing my mom again. She was my safety net.

While praying, I suddenly felt a hand touch my shoulder from behind, and I heard a voice that said, "Your mom will be alright!" I felt that warm touch physically. I heard the voice, but I can't remember now if I heard it literally like I would hear a person. All I know is that I heard it clearly.

This was not a phrase my brain made up in distress. It was real. Everything about me changed at that moment. Sorrow turned to joy. I could not help but feel like nothing had happened. This was beyond understanding.

I went downstairs. Everyone was in tears, but I began to try and convince them, "Stop crying. Jesus told me that Mom would be okay. Just stop crying." The relatives marveled at the change in me. The things I kept saying sounded so strange.

My mom indeed died. The doctor confirmed it after examining her. The nurses put my mom on a cart, rolled the white sheet over her body, and pushed her out into the hallway. By law, they had to wait two hours before taking a dead body to the morgue. After two hours, when they checked my mom's body again, they noticed her eyebrow twitching—a sign of life.

The nurses quickly brought her back and began to work to revive my mom. She came back to life. Mom lost a lot of blood, but she was breathing. Some weeks later, during a check-up appointment, the doctor came in and told my mom, "I've been doing this for a long time. Let me tell you one thing: no one comes back from where you came from." At the end of the appointment, he stopped my mom and repeated, "I'm telling you. No one comes back from where you came from."

Several weeks after those horrifying events, Mom finally came home. I was ecstatic. Jesus kept His promise. I was so happy.

The next day, walking home from school, I felt so joyful. I was jumping and skipping in the middle of an empty street. Cars would drive by very rarely through the village in the nineties. I could not wait to see my mom at home.

All of a sudden, a man appeared right beside me. It was Jesus. He took my backpack full of thick books and put it over His shoulder. He took me by my hand and continued with me, jumping and skipping in the middle of the street. I still remember exactly where it happened—right alongside our church property.

I said, "Jesus, You have saved my mom. You brought her back to life. You are so good, but how can I thank You for it?"

Jesus answered, "The time will come when you will thank Me. I will instill in you the love for Me, and I will send you to many tribes and nations around the world so you can tell them about Me."

I don't recall how He disappeared, but that was it. So I quickly ran home to tell my mom what had happened. Many other relatives were there and heard me share it. As a little kid, I shared everything that happened and forgot about it.

Eleven years later, at eighteen, I was on my first missionary trip to India. Later, I flew to Tanzania, Ethiopia, and other countries. The

Lord has kept His word. I believe that my missionary experience was only a glimpse into what Jesus still wants to accomplish through me.

I share this story to encourage you that Jesus is still the same. Just like He was yesterday in the Old Testament, He is the same today in the New Testament, and He will be forever the same tomorrow in eternity.

Don't get it mistaken. Just because Jesus is always the same does not mean He never moves. He is stirring up the church to start making conscious steps to prepare herself for His grand physical appearance at the end of the age.

BAD REPUTATION

How about us as the modern church, the spiritual body of Christ? Do we anxiously wait for Jesus today? Not speaking of specific people or organizations, but as a whole, the global church of Jesus Christ—do we expect Him to come soon just like the heroes of faith and the first church did? Do we live as the Bride is described?

I'm sure most of the believers would answer, "Yes!" But is it so? How often is it on our lips? How often is it part of our subjects or studies?

Being born into a Christian family, going through Sunday school, preteen ministry, youth ministry, and church leadership, I have heard countless views concerning the second coming of Jesus.

Many say, "See, the first church waited and waited for Jesus to come again, and nothing happened. Did Jesus ever come back? The first church kind of made a fool of themselves."

Others argue, "There are Bible verses that say this generation shall not pass before Jesus will come back. Yet here we are two thousand years later. Nothing happened. This subject is too confusing."

Even a better argument, "We need to build the church in such a

> **We have driven Christianity into a logic-based system, not a spirit-led organism.**

way as if Jesus will not return for another thousand years." It suggests dedication and perseverance. But is it a biblically sound statement?

Somehow, we have driven Christianity into a logic-based system, not a spirit-led organism.

> Beloved, I now write to you this second epistle (in both of which I stir up your pure minds by way of reminder), that you may be mindful of the words which were spoken before by the holy prophets, and of the commandment of us, the apostles of the Lord and Savior, knowing this first: that scoffers will come in the last days, walking according to their own lusts, and saying, "Where is the promise of His coming? For since the fathers fell asleep, all things continue as they were from the beginning of creation."
>
> **2 Peter 3:1–4 (NKJV)**

The modern church may believe that Jesus is coming back one day, but definitely not in their lifetime. They don't want to get burned like the fathers did, claiming Jesus would come soon but dying without seeing it come to pass. And life goes on. Many think the rapture is still very far away from happening. This is whom Peter calls "scoffers." Ouch.

I understand the skepticism. In recent decades, many wackos tried to foretell the coming of Jesus using specific dates. People took it seriously even though the Bible states explicitly that only the Father knows the time (Matthew 24:36).

Of course, none of those dates came to pass, but the damage brought upon the church was real. Christianity became a laughing stock in the media. In the church, even good believers would start avoiding the topic altogether.

Some church leaders suggest not to go into eschatology. It has too many uncertainties. Whatever is bound to happen will happen. One may become a weirdo in the eyes of the public for talking too much about it. "Just let it unfold on its own," they say.

They would say, "Let it happen when it happens. Just stay faithful. You can't do anything about it anyway. Jesus Himself doesn't know when it will happen, so leave the topic alone."

Yet, reading the book of Hebrews, I found that there is a lot more to this. This topic is critically important if we want to see a church that is awake and devoted to the Lord.

"Build the church as if Jesus won't return for another thousand years." I don't think this is viable way of thinking. What if we built the church as if Jesus would return tomorrow? Would we be more effective? Would we be more motivated? What would happen to our generosity, dedication, and fear of man? What would we do about our priorities if we built His church as if He is coming tomorrow?

CLEANING THE HOUSE

> But, beloved, do not forget this one thing, that with the Lord one day is as a thousand years, and a thousand years as one day. The Lord is not slack concerning His promise, as some count slackness, but is longsuffering toward us, not willing that any should perish but that all should come to repentance.
>
> **2 Peter 3:8–9 (NKJV)**

How will you prepare your house if the guests are coming soon?

Sometimes, my wife and I end up with a very messy house. We have four little kids, and there are days when we are just wiped out.

I remember one day in our lives. The house was a mess. The dirty dishes were up to the ceiling. The kids' stinky socks were everywhere, even on door handles. The living room rug was full of crumbs; you could mistake it for a sandbox.

We had zero strength and motivation to clean anything up whatsoever. It felt like nothing could get us on our feet. We were simply exhausted. Then this thought crept in: *Let's invite someone over for dinner*. And so we gave our friends a holler.

Within an hour, the house was sparkling clean. Knowing that guests were coming gave us a tremendous boost of energy to get our bottoms off the couch. The guests came and complimented our clean-looking house. Little did they know how our heels were on fire as we ran around cleaning up the place in an accelerated mode.

It is the same way with Jesus. When you are expecting Him at any moment, your zeal towards God changes. The priorities shift. You get inspired to go the extra mile.

This idea helps us to deal differently with all life's affairs. Being convinced of a quickly approaching return of Christ changes how we deal with finances, employees, spouses, arguments, etc. Throughout the entire Bible, this core motivator is vividly noticed.

> **The entire human history is a history of anticipation.**

If we take over six thousand years of human history, men of faith have always been in the expectation mode. They kept on waiting and waiting and waiting. It was only for three and a half years when there was rest. The entire human history is a history of anticipation. First for the coming of Jesus, now for His second coming.

I don't think millions of people throughout history were mistaken. It is tempting to say they shouldn't have waited because they did not get what they longed for. They would have looked smarter, living regular lives and not hallucinating about something so many before them were wrong about.

What if it was all a profound example to follow? What if there was no mistake but a pattern for the humble—to live by faith pleasing to God?

> But the Day of the Lord will come as a thief in the night... looking for and hastening the coming of the day of God, because of which the heavens will be dissolved, being on fire, and the elements will melt with fervent heat? Nevertheless we, according to His promise, look for new heavens and a new earth in which righteousness dwells.
>
> **2 Peter 3:10; 12–13 (NKJV)**

Unfortunately, the trend of the modern church seems to be the opposite of what the apostle Peter was calling the believers to. Instead of being driven by eternity and doing everything possible to bring the Day of the Lord closer, Christianity is lost in the earthly realm of the flesh.

THE ORIGINAL DEFINITION OF THE CHURCH

Before going any further, it is vital to sync our understanding of the church. Let's re-establish the definition as it was given in the beginning at the very inception.

What comes to your mind when you hear the word "church"? Is it a building, a name, a denomination, a stage, a well-known pastor, a Sunday service, or a live stream?

None of these things ever defined the first church. In the beginning, the first church never had buildings, trendy names, a non-profit and tax-exempt status, or shows with celebrity preachers. The modern definition of the church is quite different, which is not good.

The Oxford Dictionary defines "church" as "a building used for public Christian worship" or "a particular Christian organization."[10] Well, I don't think they grabbed this from the Bible.

The original church was defined by its people. The first church was great because of its people, and when it was bad, it was also solely because of the people. An outdated building could not make the church poor. A low attendance could not ruin the church. An old, smelly carpet, a dead microphone, lack of parking space, absence of Sunday school—none of these could affect the church because it is not defined by any of that.

The first church met in various places, including the catacombs, and it remained a church. When only two or three would gather, it remained a church.

This is a hard idea to swallow today. We are used to associating the church with things more than with people. Francis Chan writes in his book *Crazy Love: Overwhelmed by a Relentless God*, "We have subtly and tragically taken this costly command of Christ to go, baptize, and teach all nations and mutated it into a comfortable call for Christians to come, be baptized, and listen in one location."[11]

> **When the church's commission is ignored, it can quickly lose its status as Ekklesia.**

Ekklesia was the original name for the church, which meant a gathering of those summoned. The church was a gathering of believers, more than that, believers on a commission from the Lord. It did not matter where they gathered as long as they were united and built up for one purpose: to fulfill the commandment of Jesus.

Before leaving the earth, Jesus outlined the church's vision and mission statements. "Go therefore and make disciples of all the nations, baptizing them in the name of the Father and of the Son and of the Holy Spirit, teaching them to observe all things that I have commanded you" (Matthew 28:19–20, NKJV).

There is no need to gather a board of directors, senior advisors, or marketing teams to establish the vision and mission of the local church. Jesus already did the heavy lifting.

No matter how you word it, every church is supposed to have the same assignment that Jesus stated above. When the commission of Jesus is ignored, the church can quickly lose its status as Ekklesia.

CHURCH EVOLUTION

The original church definition with its name and practices was slowly redefined in the third century when the Roman Emperor Constantine legalized Christianity and ended the three-hundred-year-long persecution of the believers. On the one hand, the ending of the oppression was the best thing that ever happened to Christianity. On the other hand, it was the worst thing ever to happen to Christianity.

Who could have known that the end of the persecution had its secret evil agenda?! Christianity got politicized, and the meaning of Ekklesia got absolutely distorted.

Constantine erected beautiful church buildings as a neutral ground for the believers to meet. This allowed him to restructure the church around the government and further extended his influence.

The Word began to be slowly taken away from the people, and the status of the ministers was raised to be viewed as more holy, more privileged, and wiser than that of the regular attender.

The progressive leadership of Constantine shifted the church off its biblical base. Freedom from persecution was great, but it also shifted the church into nominalism. Miracles ceased. The pure Word was no longer presented. The kingdom of God was no longer like yeast, which grows under pressure (Matthew 13:31–33).

Almost two thousand years have passed since then, yet much of the same Constantine-era church structure is still easily recognizable in the modern church.

Recently, I heard one pastor preach to his congregation, "I, as a pastor, don't fully understand grace. How can you ever get a grasp on it?" Another pastor here in the Portland area openly teaches that only pastors are given the divine right to interpret the scripture to the flock. Thanks, Constantine. Facepalm.

The modern church across denominations raises monumental buildings. Corporate-like structures govern her, but the model left for us by the Holy Spirit, to a large degree, is abandoned.

"Now you are Christ's body, and individually members of it" (1 Corinthians 12:27, NASB). When I say "church," I don't see a building. I see a group of believers. In Ephesus, there were twelve of them (Acts 19). In Jerusalem, there were tens of thousands. I wonder how they gathered being illegal and without a building. I wonder how many small groups they had to meet daily throughout the city. Homes in those days were much smaller than what we are used to in the United States.

The revival in the book of Acts was a much bigger organizational issue than what we may have to deal with today. Yet, the church relied not on the organizational skills but on the Holy Spirit to guide them. Every issue was solved through prayer, fasting, and the Word.

DEFINING PRACTICES

On a practical level, there were three things that defined the first church. They practiced it consistently—fellowship, communion, and prayer. "And they continued steadfastly in the apostles' doctrine and fellowship, in the breaking of bread, and in prayers" (Acts 2:42, NKJV). They did it daily. There are at least thirty cross-reference mentions of these practices done by the church.

> So continuing daily with one accord in the temple, and breaking bread from house to house, they ate their food with gladness and simplicity of heart, praising God and having favor with all the people. And the Lord added to the church daily those who were being saved.
> **Acts 2:46–47 (NKJV)**

How can we get people saved daily and not only during the Sunday morning service? Be the church daily. You cannot live a double life if you are a church daily. It is much harder to be hypocritical when your daily life is exposed to other believers.

I am far from this image of the church, but I aspire to live by the example left for us in the Bible. I feel like the three things desperately lacking in the modern church are the very same things the first church was founded on—fellowship, communion, and prayer.

One of the biggest complaints that can be heard today is the lack of friendliness and connection in the churches. Newcomers are having difficulty identifying with the community. Putting people into small groups to do life together is one of the hardest tasks. Everyone comes together on a Sunday but stays distant, keeping their personal life out of the church.

COVID intensified this issue even further. People are avoiding connection. If some can meet in their groups, they are often unwilling to invite anybody new lest they disturb the vibe.

The daily communion is a painful issue, too. Most of the churches globally do it only once a month. Many churches teach that only ordained ministers are allowed to distribute it. They say that if there is no one around, you cannot take communion alone. Some teach that kids cannot receive communion until they are water-baptized. The kids must wait until they grow up to be introduced to this idea. Show that to me in the Bible.

The teaching on communion itself is very shallow. There is no fresh revelation. Most of the churches I visited during communion Sunday would cite the same Bible verse every time. They usually quote 1 Corinthians 11:23.

Isn't the entire Bible about Jesus and what He has done on the cross? Yet somehow, there is no fresh revelation besides the same passage from the apostle Paul. I in no way am diminishing what Paul wrote. I am calling people to see that there is so much more to discover about Jesus in the Bible.

I won't even go deeper into the teaching that the bread and the wine are only a symbol of the body and the blood. If they are nothing but a symbol, then how could my mom be healed of cancer while taking communion? How could I have gotten up from being close to death right after taking communion?

In Mark 14:22 (NKJV), Jesus Himself said, "Take, eat; this is My body." Then He took the cup and said, "This is My blood of the new covenant, which is shed for many" (Mark 14:24, NKJV).

Benny Hinn writes in his book called *The Blood*, "Whenever we have communion, we are having communion with the Lord. When we celebrate the Lord's supper, He Himself comes."[12] In the natural, this may still be the bread and the wine, but in the spiritual, they are the body and the blood of Jesus. This is why communion brings so much of the miraculous.

And prayer?! Where do I even begin? How is the prayer ministry in your church? How are those midweek services going?

The most boring announcement always seems to be about the prayer meeting. Not to worry, the modern church came up with an elaborate solution. They called it a worship night. Brilliant minds figured that people were much more willing to come to sing songs than to pray. Maybe so, but God said, "My house will be called a house of prayer" (Matthew 21:13, NIV). Not a house of worship.

> **We will be as effective as the first church when we do what the first church did.**

Leonard Ravenhill writes, "If you want to know how popular a church is, you go Sunday morning. If you want to know how popular the preacher is, you go Sunday night. If you want to know how popular God is, you go to the prayer meeting—and He loses every time."[13]

Let's say you made it to the prayer meeting. Many of those meetings turn into houses of preaching very quickly. After a thirty-minute introduction to why we should pray, everyone prays for a few minutes. Then, we give it up to the worship leader, whose job is to keep the prayer from feeling like a drag. Before you know it, the hour is gone, and the prayer service is over. Those five people can go home now.

Can we ever get back to the beginning? In His mercy, God permits certain deviations, but it does not mean He is happy about it. Just like Jesus said in Matthew 19:8, "It was not so in the beginning."

I am not saying everything about the modern church is bad. God uses the church mightily. The church has done much good in the past decades and even the last two centuries. I am addressing the specific unbiblical things the church is practicing so that we can be closer to the intended image Jesus had set for us.

Jesus came to restore us to live the way God intended for us to live in the beginning. I believe He will also restore His church to be the church as He built it in the beginning. We will be as effective as the first church when we do what the first church did.

DOES THE MODERN CHURCH ANTICIPATE JESUS?

Though not pleasant, I want to discuss the condition of the modern church as it has been revealed to me. It is not an easy topic because the current outlook is not great.

It brings tears to my eyes to say that the modern church does not live in the expectancy of Jesus. She is not ready for His return.

As I make my case in the following chapters, what I desire the most is for these truths to move your heart toward repentance and not self-defense. We all have things to work out, blind spots to recognize, and ways to grow in our spirituality.

I want to clarify that I am not writing about the entire church and all the believers globally. I am writing to whoever needs to get back on track with the biblical blueprint of faith.

The church that lives by the original standards also exists today. She lives by the Word and is filled with believers who stand firm on the Word and move in the power of the Holy Spirit. But one must be blind not to see the Ekklesia group is not a majority here in the

West. They are a remnant. I pray that this book will help the rows of the remnant be filled with more radical, sold-out-for-Jesus believers.

In writing this, I am not trying to pick on any specific organizations, denominations, or local churches. I am not pointing a finger at anyone but rather at certain ideas.

I am writing this to every believer and the body of Christ. In doing so, I strive to be obedient to the Word, which encourages me to do the following:

> Herald and preach the Word! Keep your sense of urgency [stand by, be at hand and ready], whether the opportunity seems to be favorable or unfavorable. [Whether it is convenient or inconvenient, whether it is welcome or unwelcome, you as preacher of the Word are to show people in what way their lives are wrong.]
> And convince them, rebuking and correcting, warning and urging and encouraging them, being unflagging and inexhaustible in patience and teaching.
> **2 Timothy 4:2–3 (AMPCE)**

This command to Timothy is given for the sake of the second coming of Jesus. Paul began by writing: "I charge you therefore before God and the Lord Jesus Christ, who will judge the living and the dead at His appearing and His kingdom" (2 Timothy 4:1, NKJV).

In the following chapters, I bring the words of correction, warning, and urgency needed for the last days. I expound upon the six sins of the modern church. There can be more, but these are the ones explicitly opened to me, and I felt the strong urge from the Holy Spirit to write it all down.

As I wrote and edited the book, I kept reevaluating my life. I may not have a religious facade, but I find the things of the flesh trying to creep in constantly. This book seeks to bring awareness about ourselves and our ministry before God.

Jesus countlessly taught people to be alert. This includes the very practice of examining oneself before the Lord. Just like David prayed, "Search me, O God, and know my heart; Try me, and know my anxieties; And see if there is any wicked way in me, And lead me in the way everlasting" (Psalm 139:23–24, NKJV).

Remember this line in a famous hymn? "When the Spirit of the Lord moves upon my heart, I will sing like David sang." I added a line that goes like this, "When the Spirit of the Lord leaves my heart, I will sin like David sinned."

Jesus commanded to be watchful, alert, and ready at least twelve times in the Gospels. All while teaching on the end-times and the coming of the Bridegroom. He really loves us and wants every believer to be a part of the Bride's company that is ready for the wedding with the Son of God. But if we do not examine ourselves, how can we be certain that we are ready? If we don't address the issues in our lives and ministry, how can we stand before Jesus as a spotless bride?

LETTERS TO THE MODERN CHURCH

CHAPTER 6

TO THE COMFORTABLE CHURCH

"To take an overall view of the church today leaves one wondering how much longer a holy God can refrain from implementing His threat to spue the Laodicean thing out of His mouth. For if there is one thing preachers are agreed upon, it is that this is the Laodicean age in the Church."[14]

Leonard Ravenhill

THE FIRST SIN I WANT TO BRING TO YOUR ATTENTION is based on the message given to the Laodicean church. I believe Jesus is saying the same thing to the modern church today.

I stumbled upon a phrase recently by an unknown author, "If the apostle Paul lived today, the American church would be getting a letter." Made me smile.

The modern church is a Laodicean church. Her problem is in the name. Laodicea means "lukewarm" or "indifferent." This is a perilous state to be in. Jesus wrote to the Laodiceans to repent, saying that the overcomers would sit on the throne with Him. This is the place prepared for the Bride. But if not, she will be dethroned and cast out.

Look, even God gets sick sometimes. He literally said He would vomit the church out. This speaks of just how tasteless she became.

"Write the following to the messenger of the congregation in Laodicea, for these are the words of the Amen, the faithful and true witness, the ruler of God's creation" (Revelation 3:14, TPT).

> **The way the church sees herself can be different from the way Jesus sees her.**

This is the only time in the Bible when Jesus reveals His name as the Amen. This name scares me. It suggests there is no going back; this is it, no second chances. It will be as He said it would be, and no one can change it.

"I know all that you do, and I know that you are neither frozen in apathy nor fervent with passion. How I wish you were either one or the other! But because you are neither cold nor hot, but lukewarm, I am about to spit you from my mouth" (Revelation 3:15–16, TPT).

Jesus says He would rather see the church cold than lukewarm. Hold up a minute. I thought being religious was better than being a backslider. No, Jesus says, it would have been better if you completely walked away than pretended you were well.

In other words, it is easier to reach a cold heart. Lukewarmness makes believers unconcerned. Jesus cannot get through to them. In this state, the believer feels self-sufficient without the desire for the coming of the Lord. He's already comfortable in his own kingdom.

"Because you say, 'I am rich, have become wealthy, and have need of nothing'—and do not know that you are wretched, miserable, poor, blind, and naked" (Revelation 3:17, KJV).

The way the church saw itself was pretty different than how Jesus saw it.

Laodicea was a wealthy city and a banking center. Does that look familiar to the modern church? In *The Bible Exposition Commentary*, Warren W. Wiersbe comments on the verse above, "Perhaps some of the spirit of the marketplace crept into the church so that their values became twisted. Why do so many church bulletins and letterheads show pictures of buildings? Are these the things that are most important to us?"

Wiersbe adds, "The board at the Laodicean church could proudly show you the latest annual report with its impressive statistics, yet Jesus said He was about to vomit them out of His mouth!"[15]

The city of Laodicea was noted for its eye salve, yet Jesus called them blind. "They were so wrapped up in building their own kingdom that they had become lukewarm in their concern for a lost world,"[16] writes Warren Weirsbe. The apostle Peter writes in 2 Peter 1:5–9 that when we do not grow spiritually, we grow blind.

Laodicea was known for delicate woolen garments and clothes materials. This reminds me of some celebrity preachers who look more like fashion icons from GQ magazine covers. Yet, Jesus called the Laodicean church naked.

The church had lost its righteousness despite seemingly serving Jesus. According to Revelation 19:8, we should be clothed in "fine linen, clean and white," which symbolizes the "righteous acts of the saints." The clothes are missing from the Laodiceans.

JESUS WEPT AND JESUS WHIPPED

The letter to the Laodicean church was probably the most severe out of all seven. Jesus is using some strong language. I can only imagine what He would do if He visited that church physically.

Just look at what Jesus did when He walked into the temple in Jerusalem. Before performing a single miracle, He had to get His house in order. Jesus drove all the thieves with a whip. Consider that before saying that your pastor is sometimes mean with His sermons.

Once the temple was cleaned out, what happened next? The blind and the lame were healed (Matthew 21:10–17). Jesus wept for the world that rejected Him and whipped the church that misused Him.

Jesus wept for the world that rejected Him and whipped the church that misused Him.

This is why Jesus had to be frank with the churches of the Revelation. It was an essential moment of correction to go on as the church Jesus founded in Acts 2.

The modern church, like the temple in Jerusalem, is skilled at busying itself, creating a feel of vibrant church life, but on a deeper level, those things are often a substitute for the lack of His presence.

I would rather have Jesus spit into my eyes and make me see again than spit me out of His mouth because my hypocrisy made Him sick. I want to allow Him to do anything necessary so I can be pure in His sight when He comes.

Grow hotter. Glow brighter. Flow farther. Throw harder.

THE WIZARD OF UZZA

Let's recall the first attempt to bring the ark of God to Jerusalem. Speaking of one tasteless move on behalf of God's people (2 Samuel 6).

Until David decided to move the ark, there was no interest in it for over twenty years. When the Philistines returned it, the ark was left abandoned at the house of Abinadab.

Everyone feared the ark. Especially after God killed seventy men who tried to touch it and look inside, it caused all the people to mourn the heavy blow.

Finally, David remembered the ark and decided to bring the presence of God into the new capital city of Israel. David did not take the time to do it God's way. He did it hastily by the flesh.

The people put the ark on a manmade cart, got the animals into the saddle, and rolled out. No one cared to look at the instructions left by the Lord. I can only imagine how the ark was cared for all those twenty-plus years. Judging by such incompetence, it most likely was neglected.

On the way, the cart tilted to the side, and Uzza, Abinadab's son, tried to assist the presence of God and touched it. He thought that his human tricks could help keep God's glory stable. His trickery did not work. Uzza dropped breathless on the spot.

Death at the ark again. Everyone is in fear again. David is trembling. Everyone remembers what happened two decades ago. And the mistake is the same yet again—the ark is left abandoned at the next random house nearby.

Uzza lived by the ark for over twenty years, yet he never learned to revere it. He never realized the treasure he possessed. He probably got used to it. After a while, it looked like another box covered in dust on top of the gold.

How scary is it to have the very presence of God in your house yet not feel its effect in your life? Is it the ark's fault or Uzza's?

How indifferent must one be? There were no elevated feelings towards the ark. It got downgraded to being perceived simply as a symbol of God's presence. Uzza never cared to cultivate the presence of God in his life. The ark did him no harm and no good.

This is what many think of the communion, a church service, or a prayer meeting. Those are nice things to do and attend, but they don't necessarily change anything. Such conclusions form in the minds of the believers when the real and raw relationship with God is not pursued.

Uzza reminds me of many of us who were born into Christian families. We know the drill. We know how things work. Even as babies, we probably learned to speak Christianeze before we learned English.

We know when to stand up and when to sit down, when to clap, and when to cry. We know how the church is done. It became predictable.

For Uzza, the ark was not so much about the presence of God as it was about religion. There was nothing personal. Maybe he got involved in moving the ark out of obedience to his father or the king.

Like many of us when we were young, we attended church out of obedience to our parents. We had no choice. We either go or get spanked and then go. As a kid, I'd never go to church had I had the choice. It was boring.

> **We cannot worship God on our terms. We must follow His conditions.**

I remember riding my bike to hang out with my buddies one Sunday afternoon when an old *babushka* (old lady) stopped me and dragged me to church for the evening service. There was only one thing worse than the Sunday service. It was the evening one. Only old people attended it. And here was me, a twelve-year-old. I could not wait for it to be over.

I'm so glad that my home church experienced a radical revival a few years later, making it a thriving church packed with youth and young adults. Many of them went on to be pastors and missionaries to other countries.

Without a personal experience with the presence of God, the church becomes a tradition, part of the culture, and a good thing to do for a good person. This is extremely dangerous, especially when God decides to truly show up.

Abeddar was different. He immediately understood that he got fortunate (or, shall I say, blessed?) at the expense of someone's misfortune. Abeddar was not going to waste this opportunity with God. He probably thought, *Everyone may abandon the ark, even David, but not me. When else can I host the Creator in my house?*

And so Abeddar was blessed, so blessed that the news reached the king's palace. It even made David jealous, who realized he was missing out big time.

There is a profound lesson to be learned here.

The ark was supposed to be carried on the shoulders of the Levites for a very specific reason. It was supposed to be carried by the people created in the image of God and separated for His purposes.

In the same way, we cannot worship God on our terms. We can only do that under His conditions. God will not break the rules for us, just like He did not do it for Uzza or David. True worship must be done in Spirit and Truth. These are God's terms (John 4:24).

You cannot put God's presence on a manmade cart of religion and expect to roll into heaven. You cannot put the person of the Holy Spirit on a backburner, get busy with ministry, and forget the One you are ministering to. You cannot neglect the Bridegroom while getting ready for the marriage to Him.

Vance Havner noticed, "The cause of Christ has been hurt more by Sunday-morning benchwarmers who pretend to love Christ, who call Him Lord but do not His commands, than by all the publicans and sinners."[17]

We now have the Holy Spirit. He dwells in us (Romans 8:11). I pray we will never get used to Him and all the ways He shows up to be near, to fellowship with us. After all, if someone thinks they are standing strong, be careful that you don't fall (1 Corinthians 10:12) in a similar way Uzza did.

MERCY OF A SILENT GOD

"These things you have done, and I kept silent; You thought that I was altogether like you; But I will rebuke you, And set them in order before your eyes" (Psalm 50:21, NKJV).

This is where the modern-day church had gone wrong. We dared to compare God to us and not in reverse. We lowered God to our human level. The NLT translation says, "While you did all this, I remained silent, and you thought I didn't care."

As humans, we treat silence as agreement. Not so with God. Loud or not, He will never approve the wrongdoings of the church. Silence is actually a sign of mercy. The Bible says in Romans 2:4 that His goodness leads to repentance, so because God is not striking us dead does not mean He is okay with our lies, hypocrisy, idolatry, and other sins. No. He is giving us time to repent.

The goodness of God draws us to repentance.

Some leaders take advantage of Christianity. They preach the false Gospel and build their kingdoms abusing the name of Jesus. They think God is totally fine with it. They think they must be doing everything right because look around, everyone is only getting richer.

What God is trying to do really is lead us to repentance. But how far off must we have fallen? When was the last time you have seen someone draw close to God after being blessed? The moment someone is blessed financially, they are difficult to find in the church. The moment someone gets their healing, you won't often see them at the prayers they were so consistent at attending. We follow the blessings and not the Father who blesses us.

The goodness of God is supposed to crush our pride so that we pray, "Lord, I am such a terrible sinner, yet you keep blessing me, you keep showing faithfulness, you never turn your back on me as I did on You. I can't handle such unfair, unconditional love. I repent. Forgive me." Sadly, God's patience and mercy shown in silence are misused to excuse our sins as something approvable.

Such behavior won't go unnoticed. God declares that He will rebuke and judge those who abuse His kindness. The time to repent is now. Turn back from a perverse understanding of God and the Bible. Humble yourself while God is still silent in His love and patience.

JESUS' COUNCIL

At His harshest, Jesus never ends without hope and a way out. He gives the Laodicean church the next steps:

> I counsel you to buy from Me gold refined in the fire, that you may be rich; and white garments, that you may be clothed, that the shame of your nakedness may not be revealed; and anoint your eyes with eye salve, that you may see. As many as I love, I rebuke and chasten. Therefore be zealous and repent.
> **Revelation 3:18-19 (NKJV)**

First, buy gold refined in the fire. The church at Smyrna was poor, but Jesus called her rich. Laodiceans needed what Smyrnanias had. It was not simply gold but one refined in the fire. As Warren Wiersbe wrote, "Nothing makes God's people examine their priorities faster than suffering!"[18]

First Peter 1:7 (NKJV) says, "That the genuineness of your faith, being much more precious than gold that perishes, though it is tested by fire, may be found to praise, honor, and glory at the revelation of Jesus Christ."

Be willing to go through persecution for the sake of Jesus. This is how you will avoid the lukewarm state of being. You may say, "But there is no persecution in the USA!" Just try speaking out the truth to the believers and the culture. You will quickly find yourself wrong. Paul wrote, "Yes, and all who desire to live godly in Christ Jesus will suffer persecution" (2 Timothy 3:12, NKJV).

Second, buy white garments to cover the shame of nakedness. This humiliation can only be caused by unrighteousness.

> I will greatly rejoice in the Lord, My soul shall be joyful in my God; For He has clothed me with the garments of salvation, He has covered me with the robe of righteousness,

> As a bridegroom decks himself with ornaments, And as a bride adorns herself with her jewels.
>
> **Isaiah 61:10 (NKJV)**

Jesus had put on the clothes of righteousness on us, but it is our job to keep them on. By our acts of righteousness, you clothe yourself in white garments (Revelation 19:8). Wiersbe again writes, "Salvation means that Christ's righteousness is imputed to us, put to our account; but sanctification means that His righteousness is imparted to us, made a part of our character and conduct."[19]

Third, anoint the eyes with salve that you may see. Stop being blind to the reality of our days. Get out of yourself and see who you are from the side, from a different perspective of the Scripture. Peter writes in 2 Peter 1:5–9 that our spiritual vision is destroyed when we do not grow in the Lord. Apply the eye salve. It may irritate you, but nothing compares to being able to see again. As you do it, you will become spiritually sharp and discerning again. You will not be the blind church leading the blind people all falling into the same pit.

Notice all of these things had to be done by the believers. Jesus did not do it for them. He said, "You buy the gold, clothe yourself, anoint the eyes." We have a part to play as well.

Therefore, let us heed the words of our Lord, who speaks to us in correction. He loves us. He wants us. This is the only reason Jesus used the language and the tone He expressed in His letter to the church. Jesus desires to be with us forever as the King and the Queen in the soon-to-be age.

Do not allow the lukewarmness in your heart. The stakes are high. Instead, cling to Him. Hang tight to Him in love.

"Now do not be stiff-necked, as your fathers were, but yield yourselves to the Lord; and enter His sanctuary, which He has sanctified forever, and serve the Lord your God, that the fierceness of His wrath may turn away from you" (2 Chronicles 30:8, NKJV).

"My soul follows close behind You; Your right hand upholds me" (Psalm 63:8, NKJV).

CHAPTER 7

TO THE FOOLISH CHURCH

WHAT CAN BE SADDER than a church without Christ? What can be more difficult to discern than the absence of Jesus in the church? On the outside, everything is excellent. All the right things are spoken, and even the works are good, but the inside is empty.

This is a very tricky discussion because it deals with the heart. Not everything is evident to the eye, but by reading between the lines with the guidance of the Holy Spirit, we can discern the presence of Jesus or His absence.

"...all the churches shall know that I am He who searches the minds and hearts. And I will give to each one of you according to your works" (Revelation 2:23, NKJV). We must if we are to be a ready Bride. Those that are not, Jesus called foolish as in the parable of ten virgins. We cannot allow our minds and hearts to be corrupted. The danger is not only in losing the bridal status but in losing salvation itself.

Vance Havner wrote, "Satan is not fighting churches; he is joining them. He does more harm by sowing tares than by pulling up wheat.

He accomplishes more by imitation than by outright opposition."[20] The big question is, how does one catch the enemy at his trickery?

PAUL GOES ON A RANT

Let's unpack what Paul had to say to the Galatians. He went on a long rant about the law, the works, and the faith. Paul sounded extremely disappointed and furious.

> O foolish Galatians! Who has bewitched you that you should not obey the truth, before whose eyes Jesus Christ was clearly portrayed among you as crucified? This only I want to learn from you: Did you receive the Spirit by the works of the law, or by the hearing of faith?
> Are you so foolish? Having begun in the Spirit, are you now being made perfect by the flesh?
> **Galatians 3:1–3 (NKJV)**

Ouch. Yep, the apostle Paul called the church of God foolish.

Paul went ballistic at the church, rebuking them for what many may see as no big deal. Yes, Galatians got some flesh going in their church, but who doesn't? It's not that bad. They are saved believers; that is the most important thing that matters. So I thought.

Galatians believe in Jesus, and that is what counts. Yes, some churches are more religious than others. Maybe they experience God less and make their life on earth a little bit more complicated. Should that even matter as long as we all believe in Jesus?

Paul took a radical, one-sided position on this. He had a very strong opinion regarding the relationship with God and the works (the law). Reading the book of Galatians, I asked myself why Paul made such a big deal out of it. We live like this here in the twenty-first century, and everyone is doing just fine.

I couldn't agree with Paul but was humble enough not to argue.

"Have you suffered so many things in vain—if indeed it was in vain?" (Galatians 3:4, NKJV).

This gets even more confusing. Paul says that everything, absolutely everything, is pointless if righteousness is mixed with works. Accepting Jesus to later return to some elements of the law was utterly unacceptable to Paul.

We are not talking about going back all the way to the law. Galatians simply took some parts of it and carried it to the other side of the cross.

"I am afraid for you, lest I have labored for you in vain" (Galatians 4:11, NKJV).

In *The Passion Translation*, "in vain" translates as "waste of time." Paul says the years he spent preaching to Galatians day and night may be a big waste of time. Let's unpack what really went down.

The trendy teaching of that day was circumcision. Galatians taught that everyone should still believe in Jesus, pray in the Spirit, heal the sick, and cast out demons, but add circumcision for a complete package. They taught that this would make the believers truly righteous.

The apostle Paul says, "No!" If you add that piece of the law, you ruin everything. I did not understand, "But the Galatians are saved. That's already better than nothing." Paul begs to differ.

Here in the modern church, we also have similar works done to gain more righteousness and feel more holy. We, as Gentiles, don't perform circumcision but do other fleshly works in the church. Let's cover some of those.

FOOLING OURSELVES

Here is how Christians trick themselves often. We do different things, hoping God accepts us and shines His favor upon us. The truth is that we cannot do anything to gain God's acceptance. He receives us only on one condition, which has nothing to do with us. Jesus is the only ticket to the Father. None of our strivings can move us closer by a single millimeter (2 Corinthians 3:4–6).

More unnoticeably, many strive to reach righteousness by works. Doing good things is great, but the motivation to reach holiness by works is evil in the sight of God.

> **He receives us only on one condition, which has nothing to do with us.**

Sometimes, this idea creeps in that if we serve more in the church, we will be more pleasing to God. Have you ever felt bad about not reading the Bible or not praying? It made you feel like a Christian version of a loser. And so you go pray for a few minutes, read a few chapters, put a checkmark, and go to bed feeling at ease.

Praying and reading the Bible is a must, but being motivated by guilt will not do you any good. Our Father is not as some of the earthly ones are. He does not play the blame games. He is always happy to see you and never stops waiting for you.

When you finally make it to His presence, He does not bring you down, saying, "Where have you been? What took you so long? I'm disappointed in you!" Instead, the Father says, "I'm so happy to see you. It's been a while. I missed you so much and can't wait to spend time with you."

You can pray by the spirit, and you can pray by the flesh. Therefore, you can do the same thing and have two different outcomes—be accepted or turned away.

Some people pray for many hours, asking for God's acceptance. Though we all should pray unceasingly, the length of prayers cannot bring us closer to God. We cannot pray our way into God's throneroom. We are already seated in the heavenly places and can speak to God directly (Ephesians 2:6). This privilege was not given to us for our striving.

We are already accepted and do many things out of that position. We pray out of acceptance, knowing God always hears us.

Pharisees prayed a lot. Jesus told a parable about a praying pharisee and a tax collector. A beautiful and lengthy prayer of the pharisee didn't benefit him, but God heard the tax collector's short and sincere cry of repentance (Luke 18:9–14).

Pharisees spent hours praying and fasting, yet Jesus heavily criticized that. Those acts in themselves are not a solution. What matters is the kind of prayer and fasting that is done. Are you doing those things to gain Christ, or do you know that you already have everything necessary to approach Him?

In some churches, people must dress a certain way to be more holy. I grew up in a church where women sat on one side of the aisle and men on the other. Dare you confuse where to sit on a Sunday.

I remember when guys with long hair would get into much trouble with the church leadership. The elders were strict and rebuked us, young guys, measuring the length of our hair. Apparently, at a certain point, the hair grows unholy.

My childhood friend, Leo, an amazing, anointed guitar player, was asked to play at a national youth conference in Belarus. This was at the most prominent church in the country. Leo had one problem—long hair. The worship band really needed him, though. There was no replacement, and the audience of thousands of young people waited.

The elders found a clever solution to keep the service from being defiled. They put my friend behind the stage curtain. They gave Leo longer wires to get hooked up, and he played the entire youth conference alone in a separate room. He could not communicate with any of the band members while playing. I told you, he is an amazing guitarist.

The problem with all these things is not controlling the style or culture but saying that a certain hair length or clothes make you more righteous. The problem lies in teaching that one has to do something to achieve greater holiness.

I understand that there must be modesty. The Bible teaches that. Some girls wear skirts so short that if you would cut five inches off, it would turn into a belt. I know, it's an old joke.

You may have had a totally different experience at your church. Lucky you. Or should I say "blessed"?! I am trying to paint a picture of how works can begin to define holiness, fooling and undermining everything Jesus did on the cross.

Bringing the law into the church meant that performance was a part of gaining holiness. It is unacceptable after the sacrifice of Jesus. This is why the apostle Paul was so radical on the issue.

SHORT SKIRT TESTIMONY

There was a young lady in the church I used to go to. She had a very unique story of coming into faith. Her life was hard and meaningless. She was alone, and it came to the point that she wanted to commit suicide. Before proceeding with her hopeless decision, this girl decided to give the church a chance.

She dressed up the way she best knew how as a nonbeliever. Unsurprisingly, it was a mini skirt, checker-textured tights, and high heels—the best she had for going out on a special occasion.

On a Sunday, she went to one of the Slavic churches in Oregon and was met by an elderly lady. This babushka yelled at her, "Where do you think you are going all dressed up like that? Get out of here! Change your clothes, and maybe then you can come back. How dare you step your foot into the house of God like this? Disgraceful."

This girl got scared and ran out. Because she was originally from Ukraine and spoke Russian, she decided to try another Slavic church.

Walking in the next Sunday, an old lady greeted her again. The reaction was the same, "How could you think to walk in here like this? You are defiling the house of the Lord. Get away!"

Running away, this young girl decided to give the church one last chance. That is it. If this did not work out in the final round, she decided to proceed with suicide. Maybe it will count against God since His people did not accept her.

Finally, this girl walked into the Slavic church I attended. Can you guess who she saw first? An old babushka at the door. The girl thought this was it for her. But this old lady was something else, "Oh, my granddaughter! Hi, how are you? It must be your first time here. Come, come with me. I'll find you a spot. You'll love it here today. Enjoy the service, dear!"

This was the Sunday a deeply suicidal young girl had accepted Jesus in her heart. What a joy!

This young lady did not know she was sick and had severe heart issues. A few months later, she passed away. She went back to Ukraine to visit her family and died unexpectedly.

The beauty of this story is that she is home with Jesus. She did not have to commit suicide. She experienced the peace and the love of God that surpass all understanding. She found forgiveness and eternity.

The issue of clothes may seem minor and not worthy of attention, but for someone like that girl, it was a matter of life or death. Even these small things have a profound effect on eternity.

STRIVING FOR THE SUPERNATURAL

We also see works regarding the supernatural. Some people who want to be healed do a lot of works to gain God's attention. They show up at every meeting. They volunteer everywhere at the church. They get very engaged. This is not the issue in and of itself. The problem is in the heart.

When someone who wants healing does all those things to gain God's attention, he does not understand what God did for him. God has already done everything for us to be healed. By His stripes, we have already been healed. It is not about works. It is all about accepting by faith what the Lord has already done on the cross (1 Peter 2:24).

The ideology of works surfaces when we think God must heal us because we do a lot of good. When the widows asked Peter to raise Tabitha from the dead, they gave a list of her good deeds (Acts 9:36–43). Don't get it mistaken; they were trying to get Peter's attention, not God's.

A striving mindset is noticed when we think that by serving a lot, we become more spiritual and prioritized in the spiritual line for blessings and promotion. It becomes visible when we think that moving in the gifts of the Spirit makes us somehow a little better and maybe even cooler than other Christians.

The tendency to slip back into works is easy for the human heart. This is how life runs on this earth. Nothing is free. We grew up to believe that the only free cheese is in a mousetrap. If you don't sweat, you don't eat.

On top of that, our upbringing can create a deep stronghold concerning the works. Logically, many parents compliment their kids when they do good deeds. If nothing was done, nothing to compliment. What it can do to a child is wire them to perform for affirmation. This invites the orphan spirit that tells them they must do something for approval. It twists the perception of God the Father.

In Matthew 3:17, the Father tells His Son Jesus He is well pleased with Him. He said it when Jesus had not yet accomplished a single thing. He said it before Jesus went into ministry.

We are not of this world. The spiritual realm does not work by the same principles as the physical realm. Striving for the Bridegroom's attention tells Him we don't believe he truly loves us. He actually pursues us more than we do. "We love Him because He first loved us" (1 John 4:19, NKJV).

WHEN CHRIST IS NOT ENOUGH

The question remains: Why would these seemingly harmless works be such a big deal that Paul goes so far as to name-calling? These things should not affect our salvation, right?! We still believe in Jesus, which means we are still saved, right?!

Being a little off is not that big of a deal; come on! Name me anyone who is never wrong in any area of their life. These were all my questions until I read this passage: "Indeed I, Paul, say to you that if you become circumcised, Christ will profit you nothing" (Galatians 5:2, NKJV). *The Passion Translation* says that, in this case, "*Christ is not enough* for you."

Truthbomb.

This verse means that if you think you need to show works to present yourself a little more holy or righteous, it means that Christ's sacrifice was not enough to do its complete work.

Wow.

When we strive to be accepted by God, our actions say that Christ is not enough to make us holy, righteous, and accepted. It means we need to add to what Jesus had done. It is us who make His work complete.

This is why Paul says everything is in vain if you think this way. How can you make it to heaven if you say that the blood of Jesus was not enough? How will you stand before the Father with that ideology if, for you, the cross was only a partial work?

Of course, we would never say it like that out loud, yet our actions speak louder than words.

"For by grace you have been saved through faith, and that not of yourselves; it is the gift of God, not of works, lest anyone should boast" (Ephesians 2:8–9, NKJV).

On the cross, we were made complete in every way. And for free. It actually can be that the most expensive things in the world are truly given for free.

"You have become estranged from Christ, you who attempt to be justified by law; you have fallen from grace" (Galatians 5:4, NKJV).

The Passion Translation elaborates on it this way:

"If you want to be made right with God by fulfilling the obligations of the law, you have cut off more than your flesh, you have cut yourselves off from Christ and have fallen away from the revelation of grace!" (Galatians 5:4, TPT).

On the cross, we were made complete in every way.

With such thinking, Christ becomes meaningless. He is just a part of the ingredients needed for holiness. You stand in control. You become the center of your righteousness. Faith becomes about you. This utterly diminishes the cross.

I ask myself the question, "Why?" Why do I pray a lot? Why do I read the Bible? Why do I do a lot of ministry? Why do I fast? What motivates me? What is the position of my heart? Why do I go to all these conferences? What am I trying to achieve?"

Am I saying you should not pray or fast or serve? No. I am talking about the heart's position as we do everything.

We have to realize once and for all that the cross is everything. It is the only thing ever needed in order to be holy. You may wonder if such a view gives us the right to sit back on the couch, do nothing, and simply enjoy our perfection. Not quite, but we'll cover this further down the pages.

We have to come back to the foundational truths of the Word. We must accept that we are complete and lack nothing in Christ. You are perfect because of what Jesus did on the cross (Colossians 1:28–29). Have faith and receive it.

Our salvation is zero percent works and one hundred percent grace. Isn't that amazing? Just because, at no cost (Ephesians 2:8).

He loved us before we loved Him (1 John 4:10). He found us before we found Him. Jesus loves us so much that we cannot do anything to make Him love us more. And we cannot do anything to make Him love us less. Christ's love for us is maxed out.

No matter how far you may run, you cannot run too far. I love the "Seas of Crimson" song by Bethel Music. My favorite line is, "Where sin runs deep, your grace runs deeper."[21] So beautiful.

"But where sin abounded, grace abounded much more, so that as sin reigned in death, even so grace might reign through righteousness to eternal life through Jesus Christ our Lord" (Romans 5:20–21, NKJV).

We can't even claim that we are good at deciding to follow Jesus. It was His kindness that led us to our knees, acknowledging Him as the Savior. "...the goodness of God leads you to repentance" (Romans 2:4, NKJV).

He gives us the desire to read the Bible, pray, and serve. Even in this, we cannot claim that our goodness motivated us. It was all grace.

Bill Johnson puts it this way, "The heart to seek God is birthed in us by God Himself. Like all desires, it is not something that can be legislated or forced, but rather it grows within us as we become exposed to God's nature."[22]

I hope this shifts your theology back into place. I hope this causes you to see Christianity as something simple and more accessible than we may think.

Sometimes, when I read the Bible late in the evening, I feel sleepy. Then, somehow, I find myself snoring with the book in my hands. Before, this used to beat me down. "I'm sorry, Lord, I fell asleep again. I'm so bad."

I love how Bill Johnson explains this. He says something along these lines, "When my child falls asleep in my arms, this is the best feeling in the world. God feels the same way when we sometimes fall asleep while praying or reading the Word."

I get to attend all-night prayer meetings in our region, and I love how they go. Some people come with pillows and blankets. Sometimes, during the holiest moments, as one person prophecies, another one a foot beside him is snoozing in deep sleep.

Religion would never allow that. It would judge those asleep and deem those with pillows and blankets as fleshly, worse than the disciples in the garden of Gethsemane. At least those did not bring sleeping bags with them.

When I observe this during night prayers, my heart is filled with joy, knowing that my Heavenly Father is so good. It is actually a fantastic feeling to fall asleep in His presence. Find a group of prayer warriors who are not religious and give it a try. Shalom will fill your soul.

God is not religious.

I mean, Samuel used to sleep right by the ark of God every night. What if he was rolling in his sleep and touched it? Would he die? My kids are like Holy Rollers in their sleep. When I allow any of them to sleep on my bed, I wake up beaten up. Samuel was a kid, too. He labored and rested in the presence of God.

We don't need religion in our midst. We need Jesus. Jesus and religion do not collide. God is not religious.

Sometimes, we work hard to do God's ministry and mess up. We feel so bad about it, "I didn't pray that prayer right. Oh, I totally stumbled. I forgot to end with 'In Jesus' name.' I totally embarrassed myself."

But Bill Johnson, again, says the Father takes these ministry failures and puts them on His fridge like a favorite drawing by His kid. This breaks me.

I have four kids, and they love to draw. Once, my second daughter Naomi called me quickly to check out her latest drawing. I came over and, in awe and wonder, commented, "Wow, Naomi, what a beautiful drawing. Is this a dog?"

"No, Daddy. It's you."

"Oh, I did not know my ears could grow on top of my head."

Do you know where that portrait was for the next three weeks? On the fridge for all to see.

UNACCEPTABLE LIE

Genesis 50 describes the story of Jacob's sons. When Jacob died in Egypt at an old age, all his sons gathered up and sent Joseph a telegram. They were afraid even to approach him personally.

The brothers wrote, "Before your father died he commanded, saying, 'Thus you shall say to Joseph: 'I beg you, please forgive the trespass of your brothers and their sin; for they did evil to you.' Now, please, forgive the trespass of the servants of the God of your father'" (Genesis 50:16–17, NKJV). They lied.

In reaction to their message, Joseph began to cry. Why? He understood that they were lying. He was beside Jacob when he died (Genesis 46:4). Jacob could have said that to him personally.

It had been probably over forty years since the entire family reunited. Joseph forgave his brothers way back then. Yet they did not believe it through all these years.

Over several decades, Joseph provided for his extended family. He brought them to Egypt, saved them from famine, gave them the best land, and secured their well-being. Through all of this, his brothers did not fully believe or accept Joseph's sincerity.

We do the same thing today. We try to prove to God that we are good in many different ways. When we do this, we show that we have not yet accepted that He truly forgave us. There is nothing to prove. We genuinely are holy. We honestly are accepted. He did everything for us. We don't need to strive but rather receive.

Because of the cross, you are complete. He does not see any blemishes in you. When you keep asking God to forgive you of the same sin over and over again, God does not understand what you are talking about.

"For I will forgive their iniquity, and their sin I will remember no more" (Jeremiah 31:34, NKJV).

Sometimes, we have better memory than God. We keep beating ourselves, "Please forgive me, please forgive me!" And God says, "For what? I don't understand what you are talking about!"

Just like Joseph cried, Jesus cries today. He gave everything, left the heavens, and was disfigured worse than any human in history. He shed His blood in many places on the road to Golgotha to perfect us and cancel out all curses.

In Luke 13:34, it is recorded that Jesus cried, looking at Jerusalem. He wept because they would not accept the redemption offered. Jesus cries for the church that does not believe the cross is enough.

We must pause and realize that Jesus has done a complete work. There is nothing to add to that. Because of the cross, it is enough for me to declare myself healed, forgiven, and set free. Because of the cross, I will not fail, I will not be in need, I will not lack wisdom, and I will not be lonely or depressed. All because of the cross.

Stop trying to reach heaven, not realizing that heaven is already inside you. "For indeed, the kingdom of God is within you" (Luke 17:21, NKJV).

We are already seated in the heavenlies. Right now, not later. What else can you add to it? "Even when we were dead in trespasses, made us alive together with Christ (by grace you have been saved), and raised us up together, and made us sit together in the heavenly places in Christ Jesus" (Ephesians 2:5–6, NKJV).

Yet many believers still try to reach heaven, crawling up as hard as possible.

I remember visiting a church in Kalispell, Montana. When everyone started praying, they were so loud, desperately crying and wailing. For a moment, I thought a revival was breaking through.

But when I listened in a little closer, I heard them begging God, "Lord, please, please, please let us into the heavens, at least through the doorsteps!" And they kept crying for what seemed like half an hour.

Such prayer is unbelief. It shames the work of the cross. This is why Paul radically claims that Christ will not benefit you with such an approach.

Some say that our way to eternity is like rowing a boat. One paddle is faith; the other is works. You cannot live on faith alone cause your rowboat will go in circles. You cannot go on works alone either because the rowboat will just spin in the other direction.

What a heresy.

First of all, no one is going to heaven on a rowboat. Secondly, faith is enough.

Mic drop.

Leonard Ravenhill said, "Christ is now wounded in the house of His friends." The Holy Book of the living God suffers more from its exponents today than from its opponents!"[23] This is so true in the modern church. The Bible teaches, "Believe on the Lord Jesus Christ, and you will be saved, you and your household" (Acts 16:31, NKJV).

SPIRITUAL TAXES

In Matthew, we read a story when the Pharisees asked Peter if Jesus paid taxes. They asked particularly about the "head tax" for the temple. Peter jumped the gun and answered, "Of course!" on behalf of Jesus without knowing much about the topic.

He came home, and Jesus asked Peter before the guy even got a chance to say "hi."

"What do you think, Simon? From whom do the kings of the earth take customs or taxes, from their sons or from strangers?" Jesus asked.

Peter is probably thinking, "Man, this Son of God. Can't hide anything from Him. He already knows?!"

"From strangers," Peter answered.

Jesus said to him, "Then the sons are free. Nevertheless, lest we offend them, go to the sea, cast in a hook, and take the fish that comes up first. And when you have opened its mouth, you will find a piece of money; take that and give it to them for Me and you" (Matthew 17:26–27, NKJV).

In Greek, verses 24, 25, and 27 use the word "pay." It is the same word Jesus pronounced on the cross when He said, "It is finished." Or, in Greek, "It is paid in full."

Little did the Pharisees know that Jesus was the owner of the temple. More than that, He was the temple (John 2:21).

Because Jesus had adopted all of the believers into His family, we are now royalty. We are sons and daughters of the most high God. You have a ring and a robe from the Father. And so, we don't owe anything to anybody. Jesus bought us on the cross by paying in full.

Never neglect the cross. Our eternity hangs on it.

The children of the king do not pay taxes. You are a king. More than that, you are a priest. You do not need to work for what you already have: the Father's love, acceptance, holiness, righteousness, inheritance, favor, abundance, peace, joy, and more.

This is where religion gets it wrong. It causes people to work to gain love, which leads to failure. What should happen is the works through love, which is love working.

Paul writes, "For in Christ Jesus neither circumcision nor uncircumcision avails anything, but faith working through love" (Galatians 5:6, NKJV).

If your faith doesn't flow out of love, it is nothing.

There are works, but they are driven by love. I am not praying to be accepted; *I boldly approach His throne* (Hebrews 4:16), coming to Him through faith.

I want to work, I want to sweat, and do a lot of things because I love Him. I know the desires of His heart. I know His dreams, and I want to be the one that fulfills them (1 Timothy 2:3–4).

Faith without works is dead, but the strength is in the faith, not in the works. Some may still think that a little bit of works is not all that big of a deal. It is still much better than being away from God. Maybe being a little bit religious is better than being a total unbeliever.

Here's what Paul has to say about it:

> You ran well. Who hindered you from obeying the truth? This persuasion does not come from Him who calls you. A little leaven leavens the whole lump. I have confidence in you, in the Lord, that you will have no other mind; but he who troubles you shall bear his judgment, whoever he is.
>
> **Galatians 5:7–10 (NKJV)**

The problem is that deception permeates the body like leaven permeates the dough. Just a little bit of works can ruin your entire belief system. Just a little bit of religious duty can cause you to lose salvation. It is not much and, therefore, seems innocent. Just a little bit of works and an entire eternity may be spent outside of heaven.

This little bit causes entire generations to turn away from God and backslide. A little bit of this and a little bit of that piles up so high that the youth in our churches cannot see Christ behind all the duties that must be performed on the way to holiness.

In the beginning, God gave about two hundred laws to the Israelites. The Pharisees added so much that the count went up to over six hundred.

It may look like a minimal addition. Maybe for the sake of tradition. Maybe to keep certain groups of attendees happy. No big deal, maybe. But is it no big deal that religion is a stumbling block pushing our youth into drugs, perversion, and disgust toward faith?

This is why Paul stresses the importance of the matter. One addition contrary to the pure Gospel will eventually destroy the entire faith system.

This addition to the grace of God ruins everything, and those who push it will bear judgment. Do not let even the most minor works creep into your spiritual walk. If you think or say something about reaching God through works, repent quickly.

Do not abolish the significance of the cross. Our eternal life hangs on it. We are founded on it.

To those who introduced circumcision to the church, Paul challenges them to shoot for an even greater level of holiness.

"I wish that those who are troubling you [by teaching that circumcision is necessary for salvation] would even [go all the way and] castrate themselves!" (Galatians 5:12, AMP).

In other words, if you think circumcision gives more righteousness, why don't you cut off the entire thing and be as holy as humanly possible? I like Paul. Smirk.

On a serious note, a performance-based church, a works-based church, is a Christless church. This is when Christianity becomes a system rather than a relationship. Paul Tripp writes, "Perhaps there is more Christless Christianity out there than we think, and perhaps its existence is first a matter of the heart before it's a weakness in our functional theology."[24]

WAGING GOD'S WARS IN VAIN

King Saul waged God's wars. First Samuel 14:47 says that Saul was victorious wherever he went. Yet, a chapter earlier, Saul disobeyed God so severely that Samuel told him he was foolish and prophesied that Saul's kingdom would end and that the Lord had already found a replacement.

The foolish church is oblivious to her own downfall, running on an autopilot. The achievements on the outside paint a victorious picture, but there is a void on the inside.

It is typical for people to judge by appearance. I remember being part of the church that just finished building its magnificent building. Many spoke highly about it, and we gained great respect in the city. Yet, little did the people know that big troubles were brewing on the inside.

Victories mean nothing if God is not in the midst. What is it to you if you gain the whole world but lose your soul? You may even see people saved, healed, and delivered, but that means nothing if God is not with you. Oh yes, you can do a lot of supernatural things without God.

King Saul knew how to perform the works but did not know how to transform his heart. "Many will say to Me in that day, 'Lord, Lord, have we not prophesied in Your name, cast out demons in Your name, and done many wonders in Your name?' And then I will declare to them, 'I never knew you; depart from Me, you who practice lawlessness!'" (Matthew 7:22–23, NKJV)

> **Don't work for love.
> Let your love work.**

Don't base your value on the things you do, even if they are spiritually significant. Your identity is in the finished work of the cross alone, period.

TRICKY WORDS

I recall visiting a local great-looking church with a great atmosphere in the service. After worship, the preacher came out to do a call for offering and began to unwrap the concept of the sacrifice.

He said, "The sacrifice of Jesus covered our sins. The idea of sacrifice itself is interesting. The sacrifice covered sins—and now we get to sacrifice our finances. Therefore, when we sacrifice finances, we cover sin." Amen?!

Everybody shouted amen, followed by a loud clap of hands. I looked around, shocked that no one caught it, not having the slightest clue of what really happened. Did you catch it?

Let me chew it up for you. What that preacher said is that the sacrifice of Jesus covers sin. Great. One hundred percent agree. Then, he said, "Sacrifice covers sin." Umm, yeah, sure, within the context of what was said a moment ago. But see how the word "Jesus" was gone now?

Then, that person concluded by adding the word "finances," so it sounded like the sacrifice of finances also covers sin because, well, it is a sacrifice. Now, this is a blunt blasphemy. It brushes off so innocently and smoothly that most audience members confirm the message with claps and amens.

This foolishness of the church demeans the cross.

I'll play nice and let Drs. Jerry and Carol Robeson say what I'm thinking, "Make the golden-tongued orators stick to the Word or else cut them off at the pockets. God's people need to wake up and stop bankrolling these agents of Satan."[25]

YOUR HIGHEST OF TEMPLES

I'd love to share a poem I wrote on this topic.

Your highest of temples
Are nothing more than pimples.
Your wide-open pulpits
Are nothing less than hell pits.

Your loudest of voices
Are nothing more than vices.
Your largest of crowds
Are nothing less than crows.

All your ways of salvation
Are nothing more than damnation.
All your versions of heaven
Are nothing less than death's leaven.

Can your love for the Savior
Be something more than behavior?
Can your view of success
Be nothing but grace?

VICTORY WITHOUT MOVING A MUSCLE

I will conclude the topic of the foolish church with a testimony from my friend. He used grace and identity in Christ instead of works to break free from the pornography addiction that tormented him for many years, even into his marriage.

My friend tried many things to find freedom, but nothing worked. Will power? Forget it. Media accountability? Did not work. Distractions? Not really.

He is a believer and was born into a Christian family, but pornography took a strong grip on him earlier in his teenage years.

The breaking point came when he finally gave up, realizing he could not overcome this on his own. My friend started returning to the beginning of his faith, remembering who he was in Christ. It's kind of like the prodigal son remembering his father's house while surrounded by pigs.

He reminded himself that he is a new creature, holy, righteous, pure, and an overcomer in Christ. That is the key word. We are not holy or victorious or anything when not in Christ.

Obviously, in the natural, he was anything but those things. Yet, he decided to declare the truth to himself out loud. He did that every day.

Even though he was still bound to pornography, he would also stand in front of the mirror daily and tell himself, "I am a man of God. I am pure. I am righteous. I am free because where the spirit of the Lord is, there is freedom."

He testifies that something began to shift in his soul after a short period. The magnetizing addiction began to weaken, and slowly, it was starting to crumble. My friend overcame an extremely tough addiction that lasted for many years, and he did it through the power of confession.

He did not work for it as religion would want it. He simply believed everything the Word promised him in Jesus Christ.

The sin of the modern church is foolishness. It makes her clueless about the end-time reality because she is caught up in performance. She is striving to reach holiness through works, making the work of the cross insufficient. This foolishness distracts from and destroys the vision—to see the Lord's return.

Instead of keeping the eyes on the prize, the foolish church is fixated on the rules. She does a ton for Christ without knowing whether He wants all of that. The church is doing many things Jesus never asked for. All He really wanted was her heart. "How often I wanted to gather your children together, as a hen gathers her chicks under her wings, but you were not willing!" (Matthew 23:37, NKJV).

When there are so many rules to follow and so much hard work to do to attain God, there is no time to think about some abstract future events. The focus becomes now. But true believers do not live for today. They are eternity-driven.

Stay vigilant. Do not let religion creep in. Stay alert. Do not rely on your own strength. Live in a total and constant surrender to the cross. Live and serve out of your position in Christ, not to gain it.

As you remain in Jesus, anchored in the complete work of the cross, you will be ready for that glorious day of the Bridegroom's appearance.

CHAPTER 8

TO THE OBESE CHURCH

THIS IS A HEAVY CHAPTER. It is directly aimed at the modern church in America. If there is one thing that will keep the body of Christ unprepared for the second coming, it is spiritual obesity. This is what causes the church to be motionless and emotionless. This is where laziness and carelessness thrive.

Jesus is coming for a healthy Bride.

Let's carefully read this passage as it is key to uncovering the sin of spiritual obesity in the modern church.

> My dear fellow believers, you need to understand that all of our Jewish ancestors who walked through a wilderness long ago were under the glory cloud and passed through the waters of the sea on both sides.
> They were all baptized into the cloud of glory, into the fellowship of Moses, and into the sea. They all ate the same heavenly manna and drank water from the same spiritual rock

that traveled with them—and that Rock was Christ himself. Yet God was not pleased with most of them, and their dead bodies were scattered around the wilderness.

Now, all these things serve as types and pictures for us—lessons that teach us not to fail in the same way by callously craving worthless things.

1 Corinthians 10:1-6 (TPT)

The apostle Paul writes that the Israelites in the desert ate spiritual food and drank spiritual water. He writes that Christ Himself was those things. In other words, Israel was in Christ. Israel was saved, so to speak.

This next statement ruined my theology. Paul writes that most of them were not pleasing to God, and their dead bodies got scattered around the wilderness. Shocking.

I thought that if I were in Christ, I would be good. If I were in Christ, I would be settled. But Paul writes that one can be in Christ and still die. Why? Because the focus is on the flesh, which always brings death. "For to set the mind on the flesh is death, but to set the mind on the Spirit is life and peace" (Romans 8:6, ESV).

Many eat and drink spiritually but do not exercise spirituality.

As the modern church, we have this perplexing unwillingness to move. This immobility made the church fat. Many eat and drink spiritually but do not exercise spirituality.

We come to church and keep on eating and drinking. We are chasing after new teachings (2 Timothy 4:3). We go to conferences, watch YouTube videos, listen to podcasts, and read many books. Did I mention going to conferences? The modern church loves conferences.

If this is all we do, we are walking in the flesh.

We must exercise spiritually based on what we are eating spiritually. Or we will end up spiritually obese. We need to practice what is preached. We need to give what we receive. "But be doers of the word, and not hearers only, deceiving yourselves" (James 1:22, ESV).

> **It is time to get up and go out.**

Ouch. We can consume so much truth, preaching, and Bible verses yet still live deceived. It is time to get up and go out. Come out about your faith. Do not be shy.

> For if anyone is a hearer of the word and not a doer, he is like a man observing his natural face in a mirror; for he observes himself, goes away, and immediately forgets what kind of man he was. But he who looks into the perfect law of liberty and continues in it, and is not a forgetful hearer but a doer of the work, this one will be blessed in what he does.
>
> **James 1:23–25 (NKJV)**

I hear testimonies from newcomers saying they showed up to church after finding it on Google Maps or after seeing the new billboard, or the church building seemed cool to check out. Sometimes, these worldly things do a better job of evangelizing than believers can.

We can be so unshakable, not because we are strong but because our hearts are as heavy as a large stone. While men slept, the enemy sowed tares in the field (Matthew 13:25). "While we have been holding conferences on theological puzzles, men have dropped into Christless graves by the millions,"[26] writes Leonard Ravenhill.

Many evangelists minister at churches and conferences around the world, but not many evangelize in the world. The modern church has been saved a hundred times already, but we are intimidated to go out and present salvation to the dying world.

Spiritual obesity gets in the way of the anticipation of the second coming. It does not live in the expectation of the end times because it would require getting back in shape. It would require to sound the alarm and get out of the comfort zone.

The end times demand dedication—a commitment to the commission. This topic is inconvenient to a consumer-driven Christianity because it requires selflessness. "And this gospel of the kingdom will be preached in all the world as a witness to all the nations, and then the end will come" (Matthew 24:14, NKJV).

This right here is how we show Jesus we are anxious for Him to come back. This is how we show that we are lovesick. We can't wait for Him to come back. Start sharing the good news as commanded by the Lord.

The end times call for the commitment to the commission.

Some make an argument that Jesus shouldn't come soon. He needs to wait. There is still so much work to do and many people to reach. It sounds so good, is but completely untrue.

The second coming of Jesus is the ultimate victory over Satan, death, sin, and sickness.

When I fell in love with my wife, Natalie, she lived on the opposite side of the world in Belarus. I was a student at an art college with a part-time job at a local church. Money (or rather, its absence) was a big issue, and visiting Natalie more than five thousand miles away was almost impossible.

I don't know how, but I found everything I needed to see her every six months until we got married. Somehow, I figured out the money problem; I don't even remember how. Nothing could stop me because I loved her, and I missed her.

What about Jesus? How can we say, "Oh yeah, I love Jesus the most! But He should hang on. I don't want to see Him now. A little later, please." Is that true love?

Don't tell me you love Jesus if you don't want Him now.

> Then I saw another angel flying in midair, and he had the eternal gospel to proclaim to those who live on the earth—to every nation, tribe, language and people. He said in a loud

voice, "Fear God and give him glory, because the hour of his judgment has come. Worship him who made the heavens, the earth, the sea and the springs of water."

Revelation 14:6–7 (NIV)

We need that angel today. If the modern church wants to live like the faithful ones throughout history, desiring to see the coming of the Lord, she must get excited about going into the world to share the good news.

Talking to one pastor here in the US, I asked him, "How does your church grow? What kind of outreaches do you do?" He confidently replied, "We don't do any of that. We focus primarily on the Sunday services, making sure everyone loves them. As a result, people just show up."

Another pastor of a megachurch in California told me that the most significant chunk of their budget goes to make Sunday services flawless. They hire the best singers and musicians in town. They make the message interactive and fun. Technically, everything is polished to the highest level. They put on a show, and that's how the church grows numerically—no need for outreaches.

Having great Sunday services is awesome, but it cannot be the sole focus as it is not what Jesus had commanded us. The first word of the great commission is GO, not COME! It's time to move. We do many things, but not the one thing that was actually commanded.

Get back in shape, church!

HOLY DISTRACTIONS

I don't know about you, but I grew up with church choirs being a big deal. I remember when the churches would be complimented for their excellent choirs. It was almost a competition to have a bigger and better singing assembly.

The same perception still exists today. Even recently, a family friend, when talking about the church she attends, made the critical point that their choir is the best. This made her church better by default. She went on to say that without choirs, it is almost impossible to feel the holiness of worship and the presence of God.

What is the point I am trying to make here? You'd be surprised.

A few months ago, I took a deeper dive into the history of the persecuted church in the former Soviet Union. This topic has always interested me because of the stories and firsthand experiences I got to have with my relatives who hold or held pastoral positions. They shared a lot of interesting stories.

I got to experience the evil clutches of the government that works to destroy the church, even in our time today. Maybe one day I can share more on that, but it is not the purpose of this book.

It is not a secret that during the Soviet Union era, there were many agent-pastors. They graduated from Christian seminaries, got their theological diplomas, learned to speak in tongues, and even to prophesy. Then, these agents were sent out to take pastoral positions in various regions.

Not many know that the Soviet government even founded some Christian institutes, inviting young and passionate believers to be their students. In the process, students were to be converted to pursue the real agenda—the eradication of the church.

Many agreed. Some refused. Those who said "no" ended up in Siberian labor camps and worse. The goal of the godless government was simple—if you cannot crush the church, lead it. Boris Perchatkin describes this vividly in his book *Paths of Fire*.

One of the biggest problems the agents had to tackle was the church's overtly passionate preaching of the Gospel. Outreaches were happening everywhere, and the churches grew despite the persecution.

The devil devised a brilliant strategy, and choirs played a role. I know you may think I'm crazy. Hang on for a minute here. The goal was to get the church busy inwardly and thus shift the focus from the primary mission. Catching it yet?

To be in a choir required gathering as many people as possible. Choirs required a lot of rehearsals during the week for the singers and musicians. Choirs tricked many passionate believers who wanted to serve the Lord into singing for the Lord at the cost of preaching for Him.

I am not against singing. I led worship for over ten years myself. The main problem I am highlighting is a shift from what was primarily important to make it secondary. Church busyness became a substitute for the great commission.

Over time, the biggest priorities became the lowest. The church busied itself out of prayer and outreach. The internal hustles became of greater importance.

The people who usually pray are elderly. They cannot keep up with the hippy worship band. They lack the charisma to be on the preaching team. Praying somewhere in the church's closet is a perfect job for them. So is the impression many times.

And outreaches? We can push the youth ministry out into the streets, like pushing a youngster into cold water to teach him to swim. If he survives, good for him. The leaders who really should know how to swim and show it in action are busy analyzing the kinds of fish swimming in their ponds.

In addition to choirs, back in the Soviet Union, many other activities began to be implemented, keeping the believers occupied with countless duties inside the church. Though with pure motivations, many did not realize they got robbed of the great commission.

What is my point here?

We have evolved as a church and got modernized. We have mainly dealt away with choirs, but the choiring problem persists. The modern church is so consumed by itself that it has no time for the commission. The volunteers are so busy that it is impossible to make it to another service, especially something so awkward as an outreach.

I am looking at many annual reports of mega-churches, and I see that, on average, only about ten percent of the budget is spent on missions (local and international).[27], [28]

James W. Frick said, "Don't tell me where your priorities are. Show me where you spend your money, and I'll tell you what your priorities are."[29]

Even the *Medium* article caught the issue: "If you asked the church what its primary interests are, you might expect them to say things like spreading the Gospel, developing mature followers of Christ, helping the poor and needy, and maybe even fighting against injustice. If this were actually true, you would expect the church's spending actually reflect these priorities. So, do they? The answer must be a resounding 'No!'"[30]

The weekly bulletin of the modern church is filled with events. Among the many, you can frequently find things like music lessons, financial institute, leadership meetings, band meetings, board meetings, and even fishing and language learning.

The obese church keeps consuming inwardly and is unwilling to do anything outwardly.

The church gets easily caught up with likes, views, and comments on social media. Worship bands spend endless hours recording the next song to keep fresh content flowing, yet refuse to sing in the streets of their city because they don't have any more hours in the week available.

Volunteers complain that they are already so busy with church tasks they cannot be involved in other things like outreach.

The modern church is so busy massaging its back that it has turned away from the world it is called to serve. She worked herself out of the great calling. The busier the church, the more active and powerful it looks.

It creates an illusion of revival. Pastors feel the need to present opportunities for the congregation to be involved to keep them from boredom or complaints. Gotta find everyone a job to do.

What does it matter if you are doing everything but the one thing Jesus Himself called you to do is avoided? Jesus asked His followers, "Why do you call Me 'Lord, Lord,' and not do the things which I say?" (Luke 6:46, NKJV).

This is the question Jesus is asking the modern church.

Robby Dawkins writes in his book *Identity Thief: Exposing Satan's Plan to Steal Your Purpose, Passion and Power*, "Think of the mainline Protestant churches that lost their passion for the Gospel and began focusing on good works. Their approach became known as the 'social gospel.' Some of them watered down the Gospel so much that Jesus was rarely, if ever, mentioned from their pulpits. Some came to resemble Sunday morning social clubs more than the Body of Christ."[31]

I love to ask pastors this question, "What is the vision of your church?"

They usually respond with something along the lines of "To see people accept Jesus and be transformed by His power!"

I then respond, "Can you kill every ministry that does not push this vision forward?"

This is where we run into a wall. Many claim the church is like a family, which, by definition, requires everything to happen simultaneously. You know, family life type deal. I understand where this is coming from. Yet, in the context of the Bible, I do not see a reference to the church as a family.

The church was created to function as a body, not a family.

A family has all sorts of people with their own desires and wants. A family does not mean unity. You know what I am talking about if you have brothers or sisters. The family model for the church is failing because it is not biblical.

This sounds tough. Let me explain where I am coming from.

"Now I rejoice in my sufferings for your sake, and in my flesh I am filling up what is lacking in Christ's afflictions for the sake of his body, that is, the church" (Colossians 1:24, ESV).

Yes, we are children of God. Yes, we are brothers and sisters. Individually, we are part of the family in the kingdom. We are a part of the family where God is the Father and Jesus is our older brother. I do not deny it. We have been adopted into the family of God (Romans 8:15).

We are a family in our direct relationship with God the Father and Jesus. Yet, the definition of the church specifically is the body of Christ.

The concept of family is subjective to cultures. It contrasts from country to country. For example, a family in India is defined totally differently than in America. The culture of "family" in Russia is different than in Mexico.

The apostle Paul deliberately calls the church a body. This is because "body" is understood universally around the world. It functions the same in every human. Knowing that the church is the body of Christ unifies the believers worldwide into the same vision and function.

The church is the body of Christ. A body, though consisting of many different and unique organs, is one living organism. A body is always united among all its members. A family, on the other hand, does not have to be united because everyone has their own agenda and pursuit.

> And He Himself gave some to be apostles, some prophets, some evangelists, and some pastors and teachers, for the equipping of the saints for the work of ministry, for the edifying of the body of Christ, till we all come to the unity of the faith and of the knowledge of the Son of God, to a perfect man, to the measure of the stature of the fullness of Christ.
>
> **Ephesians 4:11–13 (NKJV)**

As Derek Prince puts it, the passage above is the "picture of the completed church." Dr. Prince adds, "The different parts of the body of Christ are not the things that we do but who we are."[32] Wow. Powerful.

"And He put all things under His feet, and gave Him to be head over all things to the church, which is His body, the fullness of Him who fills all in all" (Ephesians 1:22–23, NKJV).

"Now you are the body of Christ, and members individually" (1 Corinthians 12:27, NKJV).

I encourage you to stay alert and don't allow yourself to be distracted. Ministry is not about doing things but doing the right thing. We are not called to do everything.

Vance Havner preached, "I don't believe that God ever meant for the church to take care under its roof of all the needs of its members; food and sports and entertainment and social life... Some of these organizations started out with soup, soap, and salvation. And generally, there was more and more soup and soap and sports and shows and socializing, and less and less salvation. If anyone had given the prodigal son a bowl of soup and a bed, he might have never gone home."[33]

EXERCISING SPIRITUALITY

My mom is almost seventy years old, and she is a fiery evangelist. She came to the US in her late forties. She tirelessly learned English, and even though it is imperfect, it does not get in the way of the commission. My mom shares the good news every moment she can.

One day, while checking out at the grocery store, my mom looked at the cashier and felt so much compassion for the lady. After paying, she looked at the woman and said a very simple phrase, "Did you know that Jesus loves you so much?"

I used to think this was such an overused phrase. But there is no such thing, especially when spoken at the right moment.

The eyes of this cashier filled with tears when she heard the phrase. She gave Mom a big tight hug and said she really needed to hear it that day. Sharing the Gospel can be as simple as that.

My dad also is a man of the Gospel. He is seventy years old now. He lives a lifestyle of prayer, fasting, and reading the Word. This is what he has done consistently over many decades.

While working a hard job in construction, he fasted every Friday. Everyone in the crew knew it since the first few weeks on the job. He did not boast about it, but it was impossible to hide when coworkers would see him skipping lunch every week. It was simply his lifestyle. Most of his crew were believers, and they let him do that without judgment.

Around two years later, the entire crew joined my dad in weekly fasting. They were inspired to do it, looking at my dad's life.

The person who was totally unsaved at my dad's company was no other but the boss himself. This man was a pastor's son and backslid long ago. My dad prayed for him for over fifteen years.

Recently, Dad's former boss called him to share some exciting news. He told my dad, "I am a believer again. I don't drink anymore and attend a local church." What a great news to hear. This is so inspiring to keep on praying without ceasing. Nothing is too hard for the Holy Spirit.

I have a teenage friend who prays for everyone he interacts with. He prays on the streets, at work, in the stores, everywhere. One day, he prayed for so many people at Walmart that they called the police on him. Now, that's a testimony of someone exercising their faith.

"For the earnest expectation of the creation eagerly waits for the revealing of the sons of God" (Romans 8:19, NKJV).

People respond to the Gospel. Share it. Don't be shy. Just be obedient. It is all you need. The entire creation, not just humanity, is waiting for you to be revealed. If you think you don't have the gift, how about using a gift of obedience?

PSYCHIC ON THE PLANE

I was on a late flight home after ministering in Sacramento, California. I was sitting in my seat, bored. I could not fall asleep, and there were no TV screens to distract me.

So, I looked to my left, where an Asian woman in her thirties sat. She was reading something on Amazon Kindle. I don't know about you, but I sometimes can be a little nosy. I stretched out my neck to glance at what she was reading. I did not expect to see what I saw.

Each page had a short paragraph or two followed by an image of some sort of emblem. The headings of the pages were like this: "If you want to be financially blessed, talk to this angel," "If you want a certain person to like you, talk to this angel."

This lady would read those paragraphs and take a minute to meditate by staring at each emblem relating to the content. Uh-oh. I quickly realized that I was sitting next to a psychic. I have some kind of a witch sitting beside me on a full flight, and I can't escape. *Somebody help?!*

I understood it was no coincidence that I was seated beside her on a flight without a TV screen. I knew I couldn't just leave this alone. But I am such a terrible conversation starter. Deep inside, I am a total introvert. One of the hardest things for me is meeting new people. How do I talk to her?

What helps me in these situations is the Holy Spirit. When I don't know how to start a conversation, I ask the Holy Spirit to reveal something about that person through the word of knowledge. When I hear something from Him, I feel the responsibility to deliver it. I also get intrigued to find out if I got it correctly.

So, I asked the Holy Spirit, "What would you want me to tell this lady?" The moment I prayed it in my mind, I immediately felt a headache. I realized it was not my pain. This was the word of knowledge operating. Okay, I got something to push myself into a conversation.

I turned left to this Asian woman and interrupted her reading. "Excuse me, this may sound really strange, but I sometimes can hear God's voice, and I feel like He just told me you have a headache. Do you, by any chance?"

The woman was surprised and replied, "Yes, I actually do." I was so happy... not because she had a headache, but because I heard God correctly and did not make a fool of myself this time.

The lady added, "Wow, I have never met a Christian psychic before! I actually am myself interested in the spiritual."

I'm thinking to myself, *Yeah, no kidding!*

I prayed for her, and she felt the pain ease out. As she opened up more, the woman shared, "My friends don't really understand me, but I practice spirituality and can see spiritual beings. I also talk often to my dead relatives like grandfathers and great grandfathers."

I was like, *Oh no, this is much worse than I thought. How do I get out of this? Lord, give me a sign!*

In reply, I asked her, "Did you ever try to talk to Jesus?"

"No, never even thought about it," she answered.

I said, "You should definitely try."

A few minutes later, our flight landed successfully in a windy Portland. Walking out of the airplane, we kept talking about the spiritual all the way out of the airport.

She seemed interested in hearing my perspective, though it sounded like she spent many more years than me in her spiritual endeavors.

I told the lady, "The reason I talk to Jesus is that He is the supreme power and authority over everything spiritual. I don't want to talk to the little guys when the most important person in the universe is actually more than willing to meet me and talk to me. When you go home, make sure you call out His name. See what happens."

I am sure Jesus came to her. If she could get her dead grandparents to come, Jesus would definitely come. First of all, He's not dead. Second, He loves her and always responds to those who call out to Him. I prayed that night, hoping that our interaction was a divine setup for her salvation.

Let's get exercising. Let's become doers of the Word!

SEVERE ARTHRITIS HEALED

On another occasion, my wife, Natalie, myself, and another friend from church went to the local mall looking to pray for people. We made ourselves step out of our comfort zones. Especially myself, who is somewhat of an introvert. Did I already mention it?

Approaching strangers is difficult at first, almost like stepping into cold water. It may be especially tough here in the Northwest, where people are colder, more closed up, and protect their space. But it's okay. After two or three times, it gets easier.

We prayed for a few people without much visible results but decided to keep pursuing the miraculous. Walking around, we stepped into a store where an older lady was selling lotions and such. She seemed to be well over fifty years of age.

We began to share the Gospel with her. She said she believed in God. She could have even been a Seventh-Day Adventist (I can't recall for sure). I then asked her if she had any pain in her body. She replied, "Yes! I have arthritis. It is terribly painful in my neck as it turned into a big lump."

Yes, I could see that bump on her neck sticking out.

"Can I pray for Jesus to get rid of this for you?" I asked.

"Yes, but you do realize this is not a curable disease, right?" she made sure I was aware before proceeding.

"Yes, I know. But do you realize nothing is impossible for God?"

I put my hand on that lump, and with my wife and a friend, we prayed a simple prayer commanding arthritis to leave her body. We prayed three times, asking the lady to check herself and see if she felt better. She did notice some minor improvement.

We got spiritually stubborn and insisted on praying one more time. During this round, I felt a shift under my hand. That big bump caused by the arthritis evaporated, and the lady got set free from this dreadful infirmity.

Those big, wide-open eyes are always priceless in such moments. This reaction shows a wide-open heart to receive the good news.

Commit to the great commission.

"Jesus healed you," I told the lady, explaining why she felt so much better. "He loves you. He seeks a personal relationship with you. He is always on your side." I reaffirmed her as she touched her neck, shocked not to feel anything abnormal for the first time in years.

Praise God! Don't make Him wait for us to get out of our seats and commit to the great commission.

ELI'S CHURCH

Let us not repeat the mistakes the Israelites made in the desert. Let us not repeat the mistake the Corinthian church made when she lost the zeal for the things of God. We are given an example, a sure pattern that follows those who do not put into practice what the Lord is inspiring them to do.

In Shiloh, the church was pastored by an obese priest called Eli. He was impassionate about correcting the wrongdoings of his leaders (his sons). He showed no zeal to care for the Lord's temple according to the law (1 Samuel 3:13).

This led to what David Wilkerson concludes in one of his sermons: "God shows us how he judges a self-focused, man-centered church. He forsook the tabernacle of Shiloh, the tent [church] which he placed among men" (Psalm 78:60). God wholly abandoned the church of greed, removing his glory from that backslidden house of flesh. And he judged it, writing "Ichabod" over the door of that church."[34]

Derek Prince quipped, "Somebody said, if you want to know the best restaurant in town, ask a preacher. Which is very true."[35] Not much has changed from the days of Eli, I suppose, at least from the recent days of Prince. Leonard Ravenhill threw down fire, preaching, "I'm afraid

Paul will look on with compassion and real pity on our feeble faith. I sometimes say this is a day of thin theology and fat preachers."[36]

We claim to believe everything the Bible says, yet we are selective about how we respond to it. Get rid of all uncleanness, then go and do what Jesus did. Preach the Gospel, heal the sick, cast out demons, raise the dead. And don't tell me those things have ceased to exist.

My friend once told me that the gifts of healing and prophecy are irrelevant for today. I argued back, "Why then would these things be written in the Bible? Isn't the entire Word of God timeless and applicable with a God who never changes?"

He responded that the miracle examples in the Bible were needed for the early church since they did not have the Bible. We have the Bible, so we do not need those miracles today. Sure, point me to a verse on this, please.

I said, "But those stories are the Bible itself. The entire Bible is the Word of God, and the Word of God is Jesus. Are you telling me some parts of Jesus have died off and not alive anymore? Why don't you rip all the pages not written for you? You don't need them."

Jesus never changed, and no one could control Him. The entire New Testament is based on the Old Testament and is backed up by it. If you will, the New Testament is a commentary on the Old Testament. The Old Testament's purpose was to lead us to the New Testament. If we pick and choose what is applicable today, the whole faith system crumbles. If your life does not align with the Word, the issue is not the Bible. I think you know who the problem is.

Just like the Old Testament is still relevant, so is the New Testament, without exceptions. Jesus is relevant today; whatever He did back then was Him leading by example. He was showing everything we can do through Him today.

Do not let such rhetoric lead the way. It brings complacency and stagnation to remove the zeal for the things of God. If you are not watchful, you will stop moving and grow obese.

Unlike Eli, Jesus took care of His house well, even when that required a whip. Mark Sayers writes, "We need a great awakening where Christians are influential without being influenced."[37]

Jesus is coming soon. He knows what His Bride looks like. It is time to reevaluate our lives, beliefs, traditions, and ministries. Focus everything on the quickly approaching Day of the Lord.

During the COVID-19 crisis, a mega-church pastored by Jason Lozano grew substantially, defying the odds. Many churches got locked, bankrupted, and emptied out. But what made Lozano's church highly effective in a terribly difficult time was discipleship based on the first church model.

In an interview with Vlad Savchuk, Lozano shares, "When the Coronavirus hit, we built our church for persecution. We did not build it for the virus. We couldn't even meet in homes... It ended up exploding through Zoom meetings. From about three thousand every week in groups to over sixty-three hundred. We doubled during the coronavirus."

Jason Lozano concludes, "That tells you the power of discipleship model church."[38]

Doing a transactional church is easy. It is like going through a drive-through at McDonalds. Grab your snack and keep on going. If you stay, you actually hold up the line and get everyone grumpy.

Doing the discipleship church is hard. It is time-consuming. It requires rolling up the sleeves and getting dirty in the weeds of people's lives. But if you let go of your own agenda, you will find a lot of joy in the hard work because you will also see the fruit of your labor.

Get active. Exercise your faith. Don't let the flesh creep in and rule your life as it did with the Israelites. They had all the right things—spiritual food and drink, yet were unacceptable to God, falling in the desert.

Get busy with the right things. If you get occupied by the things that keep you from serving God through prayer and serving people through the great commission, you will get deceived. This will quickly cause you to grow obese and spiritually self-centered, rendering yourself ineffective.

Go and make disciples. Live out your faith. Your righteous acts will prepare you for the wedding feast. They will make up your wedding dress itself. As you move to live by the Spirit, you will be pleasing to the Lord and find yourself with a great reward in heaven.

"For the Son of Man will come in the glory of His Father with His angels, and then He will reward each according to his works" (Matthew 16:27, NKJV).

CHAPTER 9

TO THE SLEEPING CHURCH

ABOUT TWO YEARS AGO, I BEGAN having a series of dreams. All of these dreams were on the same topic. God does this with me when He really wants to grab my attention because I don't always take my dreams seriously. But let me tell you, when the same dream repeats over five times, it is serious. When this happens, I just pray, "Sorry, Lord. I'm listening now."

In this series of dreams, I saw quickly approaching tsunami waves. They were enormous, higher than skyscrapers. In addition, I saw Navy ships. I saw war-related actions taking place. While all of that commotion was happening, I saw many people oblivious to what was happening around them.

Some did not pay attention to the tsunami swiftly approaching on the horizon. Others were in a deep sleep: on vacation, in their homes, and even on the Navy ships.

I understood that the tsunamis I saw were all too big to escape. They were growing higher and higher on the way to cover the entire globe. I understood that if one did not know the enormous waves were coming, it would be too late to run. If someone knew ahead of time, then maybe they had a chance.

Seeing all these dreams, I told my wife that the next global issue after COVID-19 would be war-related. Next thing you know, the war broke out in Ukraine, now affecting the entire world.

In one dream, a tsunami wave covered the entire city. Even the skyscrapers went underwater. These waves would not retract, and people had to learn to live in a new world that was submerged underwater. I saw people in the training camps learning to fight sea monsters that had now become part of their underworld. Those beasts reminded me of the Leviathan—the devil waging war against the church and the people of God.

These dreams had been confirmed countless times by other believers who saw similar visions. I heard many prominent preachers prophesying of the same thing. A new reality is coming. A great shift will occur, requiring true faith to live victorious lives. The future will have no room for the middle.

I want to sound the alarm. I pray this book wakes somebody up. Look around. Stop daydreaming that things will get back to how they used to be. Don't be delusional. Spiritual slumber is a critical issue I cannot stress enough.

A GREAT APOSTASY

Derek Prince writes in his book *Shaping History Through Prayer and Fasting*, "The church stands as the barrier to the accomplishment of Satan's supreme ambition, which is to gain dominion over the whole earth."[39]

In an effort to break this barrier, the devil will send a great apostasy upon the church of God.

> Now, brethren, concerning the coming of our Lord Jesus Christ and our gathering together to Him, we ask you, not to be soon shaken in mind or troubled, either by spirit or by word or by letter, as if from us, as though the day of Christ had come. Let no one deceive you by any means; for that Day will not come unless the falling away comes first, and the man of sin is revealed, the son of perdition.
>
> **2 Thessalonians 2:1–3 (NKJV)**

It is all a part of Satan's plan to break through the wall that keeps him out. This wall is the living church.

"And now you know what is restraining, that he may be revealed in his own time. For the mystery of lawlessness is already at work; only He who now restrains will do so until He is taken out of the way" (2 Thessalonians 2:6–7, NKJV).

Unfortunately, many believers are giving into it, realizing this prophesied apostasy at the end of the age.

> The coming of the lawless one is according to the working of Satan, with all power, signs, and lying wonders, and with all unrighteous deception among those who perish, because they did not receive the love of the truth, that they might be saved. And for this reason God will send them strong delusion, that they should believe the lie, that they all may be condemned who did not believe the truth but had pleasure in unrighteousness.
>
> **2 Thessalonians 2:9–12 (NKJV)**

We live in the age of this great abandonment of faith. Of course, if you only follow the churches and ministries on fire, you will think Christianity is doing great. But overall, here in the West, Christianity is in decline.

A report by the *Pew Research Center* and the *General Social Survey* found that the large number of people in the US who practice Christianity is declining.[40] The religion's demographic had declined since the nineties, with many adults transitioning to identify as atheists, agnostics, or "nothing in particular."

In the early nineties, about 90 percent of people in the US identified as Christians. In 2020, Christians comprised about 64 percent of the US adults and children. Meanwhile, those not associated with a religion have grown from 16 percent in 2007 to 30 percent in 2020.

The truth is under attack, unlike ever before. Even many church leaders, pastors, and bishops are now questioning the foundational truths of the Bible.

This may be a spiritual crisis that is quickly taking Christianity back to the dark era. Only 37 percent of US pastors hold a biblical worldview.[41] More than one-third of senior pastors in the USA believe that being a good person can earn you salvation.[42] Many believe there is more than one way to heaven.

Some Christians even teach that Jesus is not necessarily a God and that He was not born of a virgin, Mary. Walking on the streets, one can't help but notice countless pride flags on church buildings today. Recently, I watched a message by a Baptist pastor, who holds a major voice in the country, saying, "The church has a lot to learn from the gay and transgender community." He is inviting them to teach at his church.

It is not hard to notice churches working with the government to push specific agendas on political and cultural grounds. I can go on and on.

The great falling away is happening right now. The church today is either too boring or too entertaining, but it is not truthful (full of the truth). We are living at the end of the age.

James Maloney writes, "Departing from the faith is not necessarily overtly 'back-sliding' and giving away one's salvation (although it can be this); but rather, it generally means to turn away from sound, Christian doctrine."[43]

Mario Murillo examines the state of the church in America in his book *Vessels of Fire and Glory*. He draws a rather dire conclusion:

"A stupor has settled over the people of God that blurs the lines of what is sacred and secular—what is urgent and what is nonchalant—leaving us with people who are not hungry, burdened, or even curious about seeking the Holy Spirit."[44]

The apostle Paul notes more on this topic:

"What then? Israel has not obtained what it seeks; but the elect have obtained it, and the rest were blinded. Just as it is written: 'God has given them a spirit of stupor, Eyes that they should not see And ears that they should not hear, To this very day'" (Romans 11:7–10, NKJV).

This is the picture of the last days. Paul is not pointing to the unbelievers only. There is also a great deception in the church. Paul called it a spirit of slumber or stupor. It means a state of near-unconsciousness or insensibility.

This is the state of the heart. Paul writes that the Gospel was preached, the truth was spoken, but the people did not receive it. They did not fall in love with the truth, but they rejected the way of Christ. Even though it was spoken repeatedly, they did not respond.

A POINT OF NO RETURN

Eventually, there comes a breaking point—a point of no return.

God is merciful. He was merciful to Israel for over three hundred years until justice had to be poured out. I feel like God uses justice as a last resort. In religion, it is the first and the only option.

When we stay stubborn, at a certain point, God says, "Enough is enough. I've spoken to you repeatedly. I tried to wake you up, to resurrect you. You are not falling in love with the truth. I am stepping aside."

Then, the spirit of slumber, or stupor, creeps in to take the place of God. It comes with a strong delusion to make you believe a lie. Look around the modern society we live in. Does it look familiar to what we are discussing here?

The lie comes with a purpose: condemn all who do not believe the truth. It is coming for those who, instead of loving the truth, found pleasure in unrighteousness. This goes for believers, just like the unbelievers.

I remember a girl who used to come to the youth services I led. She was so excited as a newborn Christian, but when the topic of homosexuality came up, she was quickly disappointed.

There is no way to weave around and say homosexuality is not a sin, but she did not want to accept it because many of her friends were in that lifestyle. Instead of sharing the saving Gospel with them, she backslid, choosing friends over Jesus.

> **They've been let down to grow up this way by the culture and a laid-back church.**

I have a Christian friend whose kid got terribly sick, and the doctors struggled to diagnose what was wrong. My friend did everything he could to help. He's a good father. He visited all the doctors he could around the country. He did everything he could. But the one thing he would not do is to bring his baby to a prayer meeting.

How must we have fallen that prayer is not even an option? Prayer became nothing more than a polite gesture. It does not make sense to avoid God's availability to help, especially for a believer.

These are proofs of the spirit of slumber at work. Any belief system that teaches Jesus cannot do what He did two thousand years ago is false.

We have an entire generation that follows their feelings. It is not their fault. They've been let down to grow up this way by the culture and a laid-back church. These people have heard about Jesus but never really got serious about Him because it takes self-denial. A narcissistic Christianity hates a self-denying faith.

You can play the Christian game until the breaking point arrives. I believe as the body of Christ in the West, we are at this point of no return. This is the decision time right now to make up our minds.

The delusion caused by the spirit of stupor is tough to break. The eyes are there, but they do not see. One might say, "Hey, I'm a Christian. What else do you want? I come to church, I volunteer, I even tithe. You expect too much of me!"

The ears are there, but they do not hear. "Hey, I'm present. I sit through the sermons. I only listen to Christian music." Those sleeping ears are much more receptive to the demonic voices than the call of God to wake up.

Many have been induced into a spiritual coma. Some are sleeping with their eyes open. It is only a supernatural act of God that can resurrect a person. This is what I am trying to do in this book. I hope to reach your spirit and speak to it.

With the help of the Holy Spirit, I want to bypass the mind and the soul and strike deeper to reach the spirit. Naturally, I want to resist this message myself. It may be harsh and not pleasing at times. But let me reassure you—it is good for you. I am on the same side as you, examining my heart even as I write.

This spirit of stupor must be talked about if we want to expose it. Then, we resist it and break it. So, let's get practical.

SYMPTOMS OF STUPOR

Here are some symptoms of the spirit of slumber. You can checkmark whatever relates to you.

- **You start feeling sleepy when reading the Bible.** I'm not talking about the times when you read it at midnight. Whenever you read it, you feel sleepy.

- **You feel sleepy during church.** You feel great on a Sunday morning. You got your coffee before entering the sanctuary, but you start yawning the moment you walk inside. Did you ever consider why? You felt totally energetic a few minutes earlier. No matter who preaches, no matter how amazing a guest preacher comes, and no matter what the message is. You may even hear a screamer that runs around the stage, trying to get everyone fired up. Your reaction is always—"Eh."
- **You always go with the flow.** You cannot go against yourself to do what is right. You cannot respond whenever the truth challenges you to live better. You say something, and the next day, you're convinced you never said it. What you don't realize is you are talking in your sleep.
- **Your spiritual life does not change for years.** Let me pause here for a second. Dig a little deeper into yourself right now. Are you closer to Jesus today than yesterday? People who are slumbering are totally okay with where they are at. If they are not okay, they still will do nothing about it.
- **You may see all the perversion in the culture**, but you say, "I don't care. It is not my life." You cannot enjoy the fellowship of the saints. Worship?! You simply endure it. You return home from church, and it feels cold, empty, and sad.
- **Here is another major one.** The Holy Spirit performs amazing miracles: healings, deliverances, breakthroughs, yet you stand unimpressed and skeptical. I have seen this over and over again, even when the Lord would heal chronic illnesses before people's eyes. Many are insensitive and are not moved by the testimonies of God's glorious works. They are sleeping. How can we not respond to what the Lord is doing?

Do any of these points apply to you? Do not argue that even though you may feel sleepy, at least you are not going backward. No, no. While you are at the same level, the time is passing by.

It is like inflation. You can have twenty thousand dollars in your bank account. Technically, five years later, they are still twenty thousand dollars. But they are not worth the same. We have to grow.

Do not be resistant to rebuke and a challenge to change. Paul Tripp warns, "In their blindness, they begin to think of themselves as more righteous than they actually are, and because they think they are more righteous than they actually are, they are resistant to change."[45]

In John 3:16, God says, "I gave my Son for you!" and in Revelation 3:16, He warns, "If you are not alive in my Son, I will spit you out."

Leonard Ravenhill rebuked the church of his day by drawing a powerful comparison:
- Sodom had no churches. We have thousands.
- Sodom had no Bible. We have millions.
- Sodom had no preachers. We have ten thousand plus thousands.
- Sodom had no Bible schools. We have at least two hundred and fifty (much more now).
- Sodom had no histories of God's judgment to warn it of danger. We have volumes of them.[46]

Don't fall asleep. Stay with me here.

HOPPING OVER HOPE

Let me talk to the women for a moment. I will read from the apostle Peter. He was a man talking to women, so I feel I can do that, too.

> Let your true beauty come from your inner personality, not a focus on the external. For lasting beauty comes from a gentle and peaceful spirit, which is precious in God's sight and is much more important than the outward adornment of elaborate hair, jewelry, and fine clothes. Holy women of long ago

who had set their hopes in God beautified themselves with lives lived in deference to their own husbands' authority.

1 Peter 3:3-5 (TPT)

What am I trying to say here by quoting this passage?! You can fall asleep when you give too much attention to the flesh. Obviously, I am talking about an obsession or excessiveness.

Jesus had great and expensive clothes, but He was not a stumbling block for others. This is important for some men, too, after looking at certain celebrity preachers.

You know, once, I was sitting in a room, and it felt like someone forgot to close the door. I just felt this wind blowing. But then it dawned on me. I was in the company of some fancy ladies. Their eyelashes were so big, like those feathery fans in the hands of Pharos' servants. Every time they blinked, I was blown away. I'm being sarcastic, but you get the picture.

Kim Kardashian can dress in whatever way she desires, but God did not call you to be a sex symbol. You are a child of God, created by the Master. What else do you need?

"But I'm trying to please my husband!" you might vocalize. If you need a fake face and bee-stung lips to please your husband, tell him to get rid of his belly first.

Sometimes, I meet ladies, unsure if they are going for a handshake or a kiss. Their lips are so blown up that it leaves me confused. I just try to keep my distance or put my wife in front of me as a shield.

Peter had to address this issue with the first church, taking it to the root cause. There was too much showing off, which caused deeper issues than one can realize. He stated that it is actually an issue of hope.

Let us be real. If you are a woman and have done all those upgrades and facelifts, what were you thinking about in the process? What was your emotional state during that season? Was there jealousy? Depression? Did you want to feel better about yourself?

Peter wrote it is an issue of hope, and we should not hop over it hoping to get to internal well-being. Let us have Christ define us—the hope of Glory. Do not fall asleep. Instead, shift your priorities and start praying. Start interceding. Your voice is needed. Do not focus on the flesh. You lack nothing in Jesus. He is not your peers. He will not judge or let you down. There is only one person to impress, and that is Jesus.

So many people have been pushed away from the church because of all the glamour. I saw many times when people could not fit in at certain churches because it would require them to live at a more prestigious level.

Some women are afraid to show up to church wearing the same dress twice. Their girlfriends will ridicule them. At some churches, the prosperity Gospel took hold so hard that when someone drives up in an old car wearing basic clothes, you know, not your Sunday attire, they are looked upon as a sinner cursed by poverty.

> **There is only one person to impress, and that is Jesus.**

There is also a lot of feminism in the church. This ideology drives many women to lose modesty, and young girls don't have a good example to follow.

I believe God calls us to the way of old, an ancient path. The apostle Peter counseled to take an example from the women of old. Look at Sarah, Rebecca, Deborah, and Mary. Do not look at celebrities on Instagram and TikTok.

When Rebecca saw her future husband, Isaac, she covered her face. Nowadays, when a girl sees an attractive guy, she goes uncovered, screaming, "Take me!" I am not kidding.

Recently, while at a gas station, I witnessed how a young girl pulled up in her car, rolled down the window, and screamed to a guy, "Hey, you are really cute!" I just wanted to spank that thing. Can't you tell that we live at the end times, people?

Peter says that modesty, gentle and quiet spirit are precious to God.

A lot of people die in their sleep. Beautiful faces, yet dead spirits. Our inside man dies when we live by the flesh. This is the only thing the flesh is capable of (Romans 8:6).

I know some men reading this right now want to jump off their couch and shout a loud amen. I just gave financial advice on how to save a bunch of money. But hey, be smart if your wife is around. Quietly, give thanks to the Lord in your spirit.

My wife is an example of a person deeply rooted in Christ with her hope anchored in the Lord. We've been married for eleven years, and I learn from her constantly.

One day, I asked her, "Where are you going without me looking so beautiful?"

"Grocery shopping!" she replied. "Wanna come with me?"

"I'll go anywhere with a girl so beautiful," was my response.

I never said a thing to my wife about how she should dress or whatever else. And she was never defined by that either. Makeup or not, she is beautiful, and she knows it. In a dress or a pajama, she is always perfect. She never even pierced her ears, making my choices for finding a gift so much more difficult.

If you, men, need your wife to undergo many modifications to please you, just repent. Start speaking identity into her soul. Build her up. Never make her feel ashamed of her body or like she must do something to make you accept her.

This is not what Jesus would do, and we, as men, need to love our wives like Jesus did. We need to lead them as priests did in the temple. Convince her that she is the most beautiful gem in the world. How about this kind of a challenge for you?

GAMBLING OVER ETERNITY

"They divided my clothes among them and cast lots for my garment" (Psalm 22:18, NIV). This psalm is a poem explicitly describing

Jesus on the cross. He was hanging there fully exposed, naked, as His quality clothes were being gambled over by the soldiers below. They were sitting right there, right under the cross, playing their games. This is a picture of some of the believers today.

They sit at the cross. They take everything Jesus has to offer to them on the spot. They benefit from what Jesus did by dying on the cross naked and in pain, yet they couldn't care less about Jesus Himself. They enrich themselves with everything that becomes available.

So close to Christ, yet so far away.

Many enjoy the benefits that the church gives them. Sunday school for their kids, community, somebody to talk to, great coffee, upbeat music, positive atmosphere. These things are not bad in and of themselves, but when they are the primary motivation to show up to the church, it is not good.

People even come to be prayed for, to get healed, and to hear an encouraging word, but they do not necessarily come seeking an encounter with Jesus Himself. That's the difference.

They come to the cross and gamble over the things God gives them. Truly, they gamble with their eternal life. What a game.

You cannot be saved by sitting under the cross playing church. You must carry the cross you're so used to seeing Jesus on. We can be so close to Him yet an eternity away.

Jesus hanged on the cross naked on the busiest street leading into Jerusalem to clothe you in righteousness. Be attracted by Him, not His gifts.

Don't outgrow the cross. It is so dear. Don't seek a more profound message than the cross. You are saved by it. Long to live at the foot of the cross for the rest of your life.

I do not want to move on to a deeper subject than Jesus. Jesus is not the beginning of the way. He is the way. I do not want to see anything more effective than the cross. It is a deception.

WHATEVER IS NOT CHRIST IS AN ANTICHRIST

"He who is not with Me is against Me, and he who does not gather with Me scatters abroad" (Matthew 12:30, NKJV).

Many times, we think there are neutral things permissible for Christians to enjoy. Those things are not necessarily great, but they are not bad either. We are so good about finding neutral ground.

Sometimes Christians ask questions like "Is it a sin? Can I do this or that? If I do it like this, is it okay?" What they are really asking is, "How closely can I get to sin without falling into it?"

Many things we do cannot be put into a category of sin, but they do not benefit us either. So, we conclude they are okay. But Jesus said if we are not with Him, we are against Him. If we don't gather with Him, we scatter. In other words, the middle ground is not neutral. It also fights against Jesus.

Jesus is not the beginning of the way. He is the way.

This is strongly represented in preaching. Whenever I hear sermons that are not Christ-centered, I get jealous. Far too often, we hear psychology and philosophy instead of the pure Gospel. These things are not sins, but they are not the complete truth either.

Occasionally, psychology can be permissible, but when spoken from that perspective repeatedly, a terrible seed is sown, giving no room for the supernatural.

For example, slogans like, "You can do it!", "Pull yourself together!", "Control yourself!" "It's all in your hands." You. You. You. These things put you in control, not God.

I once heard a sermon in which the preacher gave the following advice. He said that if you come home from work frustrated, don't leave the car and go to your family all angry. Sit in your car, calm yourself down, think about your family and the good things, and when you are calmed down, get out of the car and go home. Facepalm.

Bob Larson writes, "Jesus never told His initiates to play mind games. He didn't instruct them to pursue an undifferentiated self that would dissolve their egos. Plainly and simply, He said, 'I am the light of the world. He who follows Me shall not walk in darkness.'"[47]

Self-centered messages can be a part of the Enlightenment movement, which belongs to mysticism. It pushes the believer away from Christ, who is not simply the best helper but the only real helper.

Dr. Larson adds, "For the Christian, spiritual perspicacity is centered in a person, Christ, not an experience. In truth, the enlightenment of occult mysticism is actually the darkness of the devil, who has transformed himself into 'an angel of light.'"[48] Listening to self-help preaching for an extended period can destroy your entire Bible-based belief system.

Jeremiah Johnson preached in his message called "The Arm of the Flesh in America!": "This is why a false Gospel is a best-seller in America. The false Gospel of self-help, a better version of yourself. We don't need any more TED talks, we need throne room talks."[49]

You decide today what you will serve. The Gospel of humanism, entertainment, or will you not harden your heart and turn to the pure Gospel of God that can truly transform people and nations?

Mario Murillo wrote, "If the sharpest mind of the first century knew to lay aside human marketing in favor of surrender to the Holy Spirit, what is our excuse?"[50]

Leonard Ravenhill observed, "The Church of our day should be pregnant with passionate propagation, whereas she is often pleading with pale propaganda."[51] If we are not passionate about knowing Jesus right now, we won't be able to tell the difference between Him and the counterfeit Jesus. He is the Antichrist that many will fall for at the end of age.

What will you do when he starts fighting you with the truth? In the desert, while Jesus fasted, the devil appeared, quoting Jesus His own words (Matthew 4). A modern preacher might have thought that guy was his biggest fan. It sounds like he had been listening to all His sermons. He memorized all the quotes. Impressive.

No, this was the word war between Jesus and the devil. But how do you fight when the truth is being thrown at you? How will you tell that the angel of light is actually Satan himself? You need more than the truth. You need the heart behind it.

Jesus fought back the devil, always striking to the heart of the matter. Jesus could easily discern how the devil took the truth out of context. We must stay alert even at our weakest. This is hard, but this is how wars are won.

Live in surrender to self, and you will know victory in the Lord. Always remember, there is no neutral ground. "Do you not know that friendship with the world is enmity with God? (James 4:4, NKJV).

BREATHLESS IN THE DESERT

The story of dry bones in Ezekiel truly is the story of the modern church, which is why I am hopeful.

> Again He said to me, "Prophesy to these bones, and say to them, 'O dry bones, hear the word of the Lord! Thus says the Lord God to these bones: "Surely I will cause breath to enter into you, and you shall live. I will put sinews on you and bring flesh upon you, cover you with skin and put breath in you; and you shall live. Then you shall know that I am the Lord.
>
> **Ezekiel 37:4–6 (NKJV)**

God asked Ezekiel if those dead bones could live. Ezekiel looked at all the apostasy, at the state of the church, and realized he better not answer. What Ezekiel might have thought is, *No way. This ain't happening. They're as dead as they can be.* So he quietly responded, "Lord, You know?!"

Yes, the Lord knows, and He showed us that there is hope, and the time is now to come alive. You can receive the breath of the Holy Spirit and be awakened from this coma.

The modern-day church is a story similar to Snow White. She ate of the poisonous fruit of the flesh and fell into a deep sleep. And now, only the kiss of the great Prince who loves her can wake her up.

The church will wake up when Jesus comes and embraces her with revival, with the fragrance of the Holy Spirit that rushes in like the mighty wind. I hope the church, even a remnant church, will soon arise and move in power and might.

Recently, while praying, I heard the Holy Spirit say something I felt very strongly in my spirit. "The thing that is coming soon is not to wake the church up. If you are not awake now, you are not ready." This phrase shook me.

When COVID-19 hit, everyone said the Lord was trying to wake the church up. Yes, I agree. That alarm already sounded. I don't know what you did with it, whether you snoozed it, unplugged it, or woke up.

Do not think that the next thing will try to wake you up again. If you are not awake now, you are not ready.

If you have felt the conviction, the trembling inside, maybe even fear, the Lord is knocking on your heart to break off the delusion, to break the spirit of slumber in your life. This is the time to repent and say, "Yes, Lord, I am waking up."

I love what Frances Metcalfe had to say. She founded the Golden Candlestick Company, a small group of ladies who dedicated their entire lives to prayer and intercession. They prayed six to eight hours through the night for over fifty years.

In Metcalfe's journals published by James Maloney in a three-volume book called *Ladies of Gold*, Metcalfe writes about this state of slumber. "He (Satan) is out to make war on the saints and to overthrow them... What a picture of the Church in this hour, surrounded and undermined with the works of the enemy. Alert! Church of the Living

God, you are face to face with the arch-enemy of the Lord Jesus Christ. You cannot. You dare not slumber in this hour. To do so is to invite certain defeat, and eternal loss in the Kingdom of God!"[52]

One evening, the apostle Paul decided to ignore the thirty-minute countdown for the sermon. He went on speaking well past midnight, even without the microphone. The lighting guy forgot to set a more energizing mood and kept the glow soft with gentle flickers. The room itself was over the occupancy limit, making a young man named Eutychus (which means "lucky") sit in an open window.

Paul kept speaking. I don't think he screamed like some of the passionate preachers of our day. It's not easy to scream past midnight. Lucky became drowsy and fell into a deep slumber, falling down three stories to his death.

Unwillingly, this boy became a picture of many modern believers today. I love the annotation for Acts 20:9 in *The Passion Translation*. The believers "view themselves as 'well off,' sit carelessly where they shouldn't, growing drowsy, falling asleep, and enduring a disastrous fall. But God has grace and power to raise even the foolish ones back to life."[53]

"Take heed to yourselves, lest your hearts be weighed down with carousing (drinking alcohol and enjoying oneself with others in a noisy, lively way), drunkenness, and cares of this life, and that Day come on you unexpectedly" (Luke 21:34, NKJV).[54]

Jesus warns us to be careful in paying attention to all the earthly things. Be careful because the day will come suddenly. We have to expect it every day, waiting for our Lord to return as He promised.

When a house is freezing, it is hard to fall asleep. You can even die if it gets too cold. When it is very hot in the house, it is also impossible to fall asleep. I remember, growing up in a village, the boys' bedroom was in the attic-like second floor under a black roof in a house without air conditioning. I'd crawl up under the bed, looking for some fresh stream of air, trying to fall asleep. No such luck with three older brothers in the room.

But when it is warm, seventy degrees Fahrenheit for me, it is just perfect for the body to relax and doze out into a comfy sleep.

> **I suggest cranking up the heat and staying awake.**

I suggest cranking up the heat and staying awake. Do not fall asleep. Do not search for comfort. Pray, fast, preach. Do whatever you can to not cool off into complacency.

"He who sleeps in harvest is a son who causes shame" (Proverbs 10:5, NKJV). We are living in the last days of the harvest season. The church sleeping during this time causes much shame to the Heavenly Father. Sad.

LATE CHRISTIANITY

One of the men who profoundly affected my life was my father-in-law, Vyacheslav Sonich. He was like a father, a mentor, and truly my best friend.

In the last conversation we had together before he passed away, Vyacheslav kept telling me about the parable of ten virgins. He was unusually passionate. It was as if he was trying to tell me something, give me a hint, offer me a clue.

I took some notes during the conversation, but after his passing, I felt that I had to take a deep dive into the parable. There must be something important for me in there.

You can read the full parable in Matthew 25. I assume many readers are familiar with it; therefore, I will be concise. Let's get to it.

The word describing the five maidens or virgins as "foolish" in Greek is *moros*. This is where we get our English word "moron." I guess Jesus used a slightly stronger word than what we read from more polite translations of the Bible.

You might drift off imagining all the people in your life who fit this description. Stay with me...

The five foolish virgins degraded without the oil, which is the Holy Spirit. Like today, we may be Christians, but stupid Christians if we live by the flesh and not the Spirit. Moros believers are not aware that Jesus is coming very soon. They don't plan ahead to be ready. They don't check in with themselves and pray like David did, asking the Lord to search them.

It is worth noting that both foolish and wise maidens fell asleep. The difference was that the wise ones woke up and readied themselves quickly while the other maidens could not do so.

The foolish maidens were indeed foolish. They tried to get the lamps burning without the oil. Just like the modern church is trying to run its ministry without the Holy Spirit. It is as logical as having windows in a submarine.

> "Megachurches boom, yet on their watch we have had our greatest moral decline. This says leaders have learned to do church without the Holy Spirit."
>
> **Mario Murillo, *Vessels of Fire & Glory*[55]**

The maidens were also foolish to ask for the oil from somebody else. A relationship with the Holy Spirit is not transferable. Get your own instead of trying to run on somebody else's anointing. Go into the secret place and stay there until the oil soaks you through.

Yet, I still argue that the modern church is more foolish than the five virgins. Let me make my point. The foolish maidens:

- Had the oil (which represents the Holy Spirit).
- In their lack, did not fight the wise ones. They asked for help.
- Were not stubborn but obeyed the advice of the wise maidens.
- Were humble enough to realize they did not have the fire. (Try telling that to a fellow believer today.) (A few days later, once the

swelling from your eye goes down, you will have to rethink your straightforwardness.)
- Knew how to repent.
- Knew where to get the oil.
- Got to the place where the Bridegroom was.
- In the end, they were just like the wise maidens. They were ready to walk in.

I mean, this is pretty good. If only all the churches today were at least on that level. The only difference between the maidens was that they were simply late.

I propose that the devil does not mind you being a believer so much... as long as you are late. If the devil can distract you, he can delay you. If he can delay you, he can destroy you.

Before starting the wedding feast, Jesus will lock the doors. He does not want any interruptions. All eyes are on the Bride. Jesus does not want latecomers to creep in, causing distraction and commotion.

> **If the devil can distract you, he can delay you. If he can delay you, he can destroy you.**

Nevertheless, the foolish maidens decided to knock and make their way in. The Bridegroom looked through the hole in the door and replied, "Assuredly, I say to you, I do not know you" (Matthew 25:12, NKJV). It always puzzled me how the Bridegroom, who is the all-knowing Jesus, could say that He did not know them.

So, I dug deeper into the original language. Turns out, this phrase can also be interpreted from the Greek as "I do not want to know you."

Showing up late to such a grand event on a universal scale is beyond rude. It is unforgivable. The Bridegroom was disappointed that the five maidens, though they had a lot of time to prepare, were not ready for this important event. The foolish maidens screwed it up. They were late. How could they? This is not yet another appointment, a hangout, or a meeting. This is the wedding of the only Son of God.

I remember being one of the best friends at my buddy's wedding. He also had the very best friend who was honored to stand next to him during the ceremony and later sit next to him during the banquet. A day before the wedding, the bridegroom asked us to ensure we were rested with enough sleep to be ready early in the morning.

His best friend ignored it and went out to party all night. He came home very late, or shall I say "very early." Without any sleep, he had to start getting ready.

I still remember the look on my friend's face, the bridegroom. He was so disappointed with his best friend. The guy was sleepy the entire wedding day. He was not in the best mood. In most of the photos, his eyes were half shut. He hurt his friend by being so reckless on such an important day.

Jesus takes His wedding day very seriously. He'd been preparing for it for a long time and wants it to be perfect. After all, it only happens once in a span of eternity.

The devil sings a lullaby using our very lips. You may protest by asking, "How?" I'm glad you asked. The devil sings a soothing lullaby when we gossip, live in vanity, get consumed by politics, live in debt, watch shows every night, and criticize pastors and ministries.

Either you come to Jesus, or Jesus will come to you. Life is unpredictable. Your tomorrow is not promised. The games are over. It is time to wake up and stay alert.

After the parable of ten virgins, in the next chapter of Matthew, we find the disciples in the garden of Gethsemane. They are all sound asleep like all the maidens. This perplexed Jesus, and He uttered the shortest yet the most timely advice for the modern church.

"Watch and pray" (Matthew 26:41, NKJV). Then Jesus added, "...lest you enter into temptation. The spirit indeed is willing, but the flesh is weak" (Matthew 26:41, NKJV).

I realize now what my father-in-law was trying to convey to me. He told me never to stop burning, never give in to complacency, never compromise at the cost of the Holy Spirit, but always stay spiritually awake. I must do these things if we are ever to see each other again.

Here is what must happen to not run out of oil:

Carlos Sarmiento wrote, "Primarily, the Church needs leaders (*and members*) who allow their own hearts to be encountered by the Lord... However, it is impossible unless the hearts of these leaders (*and members*) are yielded to fulfilling the great commandment."[56]

Then Sarmiento highlights the three heart issues God emphasized to him in a visitation: intimacy with the eternal godhead, the kingdom-of-God lifestyle, and the end-time urgency, which is a primary focus of his book as it is with mine.

Jesus dying on the cross was not the end of the redemption story. It was only a culmination, after which the story led to the resolution. We are still in the process of that, nearing the very end—the wedding with the Bridegroom.

The goal of the entire redemption story is the wedding. Getting saved was only the middle part. I am so excited that we are nearing the resolution. You and I have a role to play in the most beautiful story ever.

LIKE SAMSON, LIKE SOLOMON

The modern church is like Samson. The church was powerful and miraculous, influencing the entire world in the early days. But just like Samson fell in love with Delilah, the church was seduced, ending up in bed with those days' politics, culture, and influence.

Samson's eyes were plucked out (my friend, that's worse than sleeping), and he was enslaved, working for the enemy (Judges 16). The church, too, was blinded and overtaken by the earthly power of those days, becoming a system of control and manipulation. The church worked for the government under the command of her Emperors.

Solomon was the wisest like Samson was the strongest. Yet, the wisest and the strongest both fell at the weaker hands of women. Indeed, like grass can cut through cement, a soft and sweet look can overpower the mighty ones.

The women Solomon fell in love with stirred his heart away from God. He went after all the gods those pagan wives worshipped.

The modern church also has a woman. Her name is Jezebel. Jesus brings her up in Revelation 2:18 in the letter to the church of Thyatira. During King Ahab's reign, Jezebel released a spirit of darkness by mixing the worship of Baal with the worship of the true God. She symbolizes a spirit of tolerance and compromise, which teaches that God's people can sin and not experience any consequences.

Being full of eternal wisdom and the *dunamis* (power) of the Holy Ghost, the church still falls at the soothing temptations of relevance, compromise, and man-pleasing.

At the end of Samson's life, a miracle took place. His hair grew back, and with it, his anointing returned. He fought the enemy one last time, defeating in one blow more than he ever did in his entire life (Judges 16:30).

I am also thankful for the book of Ecclesiastes. At least for the fact that it tells us Solomon made a comeback. Some other indications in the book of Chronicles imply his repentance. In the end, he gave all glory to God and worshipped Him. "Let us hear the conclusion of the whole matter: Fear God and keep His commandments, For this is man's all. For God will bring every work into judgment, Including every secret thing, Whether good or evil" (Ecclesiastes 12:13–14, NKJV).

Their examples give a prophetic hope that the same will happen with the end-time church. She will come back to her first love. Politics, wealth, relevance, and other temptations will no longer attract her. She will come back fully devoted to the One.

I see the remnant rising right now. They are rising out of the prison of religion. They are not satisfied with just churchgoing and song-singing. They want the real deal. They want the real Jesus. They want to see heaven on earth, just like the Bible promises. And they are willing to pay for it.

What is most exciting is that they are getting it. By the grace of God that is so abundant in these last days, miracles flow, cancer is dying, bondages break, and bodies get healed. It is happening everywhere; you just have to look in the right direction. The end time will be glorious, and I pray to be a part of it. I want to waste my life on Jesus and later find myself holding His hand as we say our vows.

CHAPTER 10

TO THE BARREN CHURCH

I BEGAN THE JOURNEY that led to the writing of this book after a dream. In that dream, I saw the church cheating on Jesus. I woke up with a heavy heart, feeling discouraged and puzzled.

How can it be? I tried to dismiss my dream, but I could not shake it off. It troubled me deeply. The Holy Spirit kept bringing up the same point over and over again. Reading the Bible, praying, hearing revelations of fellow believers, listening to the prophetic voices online—everything proved the same point—the church is in a severe situation.

I began to study the topic, dive deeper into the Word, and keep my spiritual senses open to what the Holy Spirit wants to say. One of the most painful revelations I could not silence inside my spirit is that the modern church is barren.

It brings me to tears while I am writing it. I love the church. I do not want to criticize her. But I am obliged to be obedient to God. Receive this message with a tender heart. Let Him touch you as you read this chapter. I believe we all have a greater capacity to cry out to Jesus for more, no matter how close we may feel to Him right now.

GIVE ME JESUS, OR I DIE

The first book of Samuel begins with a story about Hannah, the wife of a man named Elkanah. Elkanah had two wives: one was Hannah, and the other was Peninnah. Unlike Peninnah, Hannah had no children.

This issue drove Hannah to tears frequently, especially when Peninnah would humiliate her out of jealousy that Elkanah loved her more. (Here's one reason God never approved of polygamous marriages.)

Elkanah loved Hannah more, and he would give her double portions during offerings. This did not satisfy Hannah a single bit, and she kept on weeping. Elkanah did not understand her pain. How could he? He had children. The issue was Hannah's alone. Elkanah thought that by giving gifts, more attention, and showing more love, he would balance out his wife's barrenness. He was wrong.

Nothing could replace Hannah's desire to have a son. She could not be bought. She had no room for compromise. There was no alternative. The greatest gifts and affections could not calm her anguish. Hannah wanted a child. Period.

This story paints a picture of the modern church. Yet, unlike Hannah, the church is more than satisfied with the gifts at the cost of the Son.

The church fell in love with all the trinkets: amazing buildings, fancy sound equipment, social media following, and fame. As Mario Murillo puts it, we became all about "big screens, fog machines, and pastors wearing skinny jeans."

The Western church got enticed by prosperity so much that she forgot about the Son. In many ways, she has become an industry, a marketplace, and a commercial platform.

We, as a church, often chase the next cool thing. We define growth based on approvals. Our preaching is designed to reflect the culture and what people respond to better. We come up with elaborate marketing campaigns and business deals to keep running. These things are not necessarily bad, but far too often, they miss the key ingredient... the Son.

"The devil used craftiness to steal our gold. We removed mass soul-winning through the Holy Spirit. He tossed the bone of getting a big church to drooling leaders. We replace revival with marketing and well-oiled, business entertainment centers,"[57] writes Mario Murillo in his prophetic book *Vessels of Fire & Glory*.

How many sermons don't even mention Jesus anymore? Even if they do, they are not Jesus-oriented. That fact that you squeeze in His name as a checkmark does not make the sermon Christ-centered.

Many of the modern messages are "you" oriented. Jesus is not the goal. He is the means to an end. He is a tool to make your life better. It is excellent when Jesus can improve your life, but when this is the end goal, it is an abuse of His name and the truths He reveals.

If a sermon does not mention Jesus as He should be mentioned, it is not a sermon. It is a lecture. We have to realize that this whole faith thing is not about us. "For of Him and through Him and to Him are all things, to whom be glory forever. Amen" (Romans 11:36, NKJV).

> **If a sermon does not mention Jesus as He should be mentioned, it is not a sermon.**

We cannot prostitute the name and the authority of Jesus, making it all about us. We should not seek out His truths for our gain without offering our hearts in return. If this relationship is one-sided, it is not real. It is transactional.

Is there anyone as uncompromising as Hannah? Reading the story, I could feel her saying, "I don't need your gifts; I don't need your double portion. I don't need the compliments. Give me a son!"

Thank You, Father, for the amazing church buildings. Thank You for the big bucks flowing into the ministries. Thank You for the popularity.

Thank You for the crowds. It's all good, but what I really want is You. You can have all this world, but give me Jesus.

The Father does not give us crowds for management purposes. They are there to preach truth to the masses. Jesus never worried about the crowds like the churches do today.

Some even teach today that you are a bad leader if only a few follow you. I say it all depends on when you evaluate the leader. At times, it would mean that Jesus was a poor leader, too. He did not always have big crowds, and up on that cross, He was completely alone.

Nothing around me satisfies the craving for the person of Jesus. I will not value a bigger congregation at the cost of the Son. He is too precious. I will not value the opinions of men concerning how Jesus moves. His Spirit is too valuable. I will not compromise the truth to avoid legal issues. Jesus is worth it all.

If Jesus is not in the center, Jesus is not in the picture.

Rachel desperately screamed at Jacob, "Give me sons, or I'll die!" (Genesis 30:1, TPT). She couldn't care less if Jacob loved her more. She cared less that she was way more beautiful than Liya. She had only one thing on her mind.

It was disgraceful not to have a son, unlike today, when the left-wing ideology discourages having kids and encourages abortions.

It does not matter what the media may shove into your face. The Word of God is eternally true. They may scream that this planet is overpopulated, yet the Bible says, "Like arrows in the hand of a warrior, So are the children of one's youth. Happy is the man who has his quiver full of them" (Psalm 127:4–5, NKJV).

The Word of God is eternal and does not comply with ever-changing cultural beliefs. If Jesus commanded humanity to multiply, it is always good to multiply. If God commanded the people to fill the earth, it means the earth has the capacity for God's ideas.

But I digress... Rachel was like Hannah, unwilling to calm herself down. She was unwilling to accept the fact that she was to remain childless.

Yet, many churches and even denominations feel no guilt or shame because they don't have the Son anymore. Jesus could not stay. The pursuit of the flesh cast Him out, and nobody noticed. Jesus will not share His glory. He will not share the same space with the flesh.

"Hypocrites! Well did Isaiah prophesy about you, saying: 'These people draw near to Me with their mouth, And honor Me with their lips, But their heart is far from Me. And in vain they worship Me, Teaching as doctrines the commandments of men'" (Matthew 15:7–9, NKJV).

If Jesus is not in the center, Jesus is not in the picture.

If it is not about Jesus alone, it is not about Jesus at all.

Without Him, we become loudmouths with closed-up hearts.

GOODNESS WITHOUT THE CROSS

Nehemiah returns to Jerusalem only to discover that Tobias moved into the temple. Like there was no other room in the entire Jerusalem, he wanted one specifically in the house of God. You can follow the story in detail in Nehemiah 13.

Tobias found his way to the priest's heart, and with the priest's approval, he got himself comfortable in one of the most important rooms of the temple. It was not some extra unoccupied space. This large room was used to store the holy bread and the wine. The priest threw them out of the room in order to let Tobias in. Who was this imposter of such importance to the priest?

The name Tobias means prosperity, or goodness, or God's goodness. Do you see where this is going?

I am picking on you, prosperity Gospel. I am not against you per se. I can see you throughout the Bible. I pray every believer prospers. But what is prosperity without the cross? What is goodness without the sacrifice of Jesus? Does it mean anything without the bread—the body of Christ, and the wine—the blood of Christ?

"Beloved, I pray that you may prosper in all things and be in health, just as your soul prospers" (3 John 1:2, NKJV).

John concluded that the foundation of all prosperity and health is relegated to our soul's prosperity. In other words, as Kris Vallotton explains in his book *Poverty, Riches & Wealth*, "the level of prosperity inside determines the level of wealth and health that we experience."[58] And "all believers should be wealthy, not rich."[59]

Biblical prosperity is not about earthly gain. It surely seems so with how many preachers present it. But no soul is genuinely healthy without the two main ingredients: the body and the blood of Jesus Christ. His body made us whole, and His blood made us holy. Now that's wealth.

True prosperity does not exist without the cross. The sacrifice of Jesus leads to prosperity, but the prosperity without Jesus leads to death. We cannot allow ourselves to use the Word of God for financial manipulation.

Jesus told a young rich man to let go of his riches before following Him because his wealth was detached from God. The rich man's money was a wall on the way to Jesus. It is something that had a grip on a young man's heart. Prosperity without Jesus is a deception.

> **His body made us whole, and His blood made us holy.**

The pure Gospel always addresses the soul. It is not focused on money. The first church was not rich. People were actually selling their stuff (Acts 2:44–46). The apostle Paul did not always have a salary (Acts 18:1–4). Some saints in the church in Jerusalem were poor (Romans 15:26). Many heroes of faith were homeless (Hebrews 11:38).

Don't get it twisted. Focus on Jesus alone. Preach Him alone. Otherwise, you may quickly find yourself without the Son, without whom we are totally and utterly bankrupt. We don't need more money and sermons about finances. We need more Jesus.

Throw out that Tobias from your church and your theology. Bring back the bread and the wine. You only need these two ingredients for a truly prosperous life.

AN OVERSHADOWING PAIN

A profoundly dramatic illustration of the true love for God that could not be overshadowed by the greatest of blessings can be observed through the last moments in the life of Eli's daughter-in-law.

> Now his daughter-in-law, Phinehas' wife, was with child, due to be delivered; and when she heard the news that the ark of God was captured, and that her father-in-law and her husband were dead, she bowed herself and gave birth, for her labor pains came upon her.
> And about the time of her death the women who stood by her said to her, "Do not fear, for you have borne a son." But she did not answer, nor did she regard it.
> Then she named the child Ichabod, saying, "The glory has departed from Israel!" because the ark of God had been captured and because of her father-in-law and her husband. And she said, "The glory has departed from Israel, for the ark of God has been captured."
> **1 Samuel 4:19–22 (NKJV)**

In the context of the entire account of the battle with the Philistines and the capture of the ark, this nameless lady seemed out of place. Yet, the story of Eli's family ends with her.

When this pregnant woman heard about the death of her unfaithful husband and the capture of the ark, the labor pains kicked in, and she gave birth to a son. You would think what a moment of comfort in such distress. No, this new mother was absolutely unimpressed.

I can only imagine how torn she was inside. The Bible says that a mother goes through great pains delivering a baby, but once a child is born, she forgets it and rejoices in the new life. It was not the case with Eli's daughter-in-law. Was she a terrible woman, or was she experiencing more pain than childbirth?

What could possibly hurt more?

This woman was of the priesthood family. She lived and served in the Tabernacle. Every day, she was close to the ark of the covenant, which was the epicenter of the presence of the Most High God. This woman knew and valued the presence of God, unlike her husband, brother-in-law, and father-in-law. She had a personal experience with God's glory. She must have.

And now she was not even bothered by the fact that she was dying. The midwives told her to calm down because she bore a son. But similarly to Hannah, this woman was impossible to bribe, talk into a compromise, and find contentment in the new reality without the ark—the very presence of God.

This woman understood where true happiness came from and could feel that it was no more. Even the birth of a son could not overshadow the agony she felt for the missing presence of God.

Her last words were not about her son. The name she gave to the baby was not about his identity or the future. Could there even be a future without God? The only thing on her mind as the soul was leaving her body was the presence of God. She named the boy Ichabod, which means "without glory" or "where is the glory?"

And maybe, just maybe, she was not dying because of the difficult labor. The Bible does not say that. Maybe, just maybe, she was so attached to God, to His presence, to the union with the Creator that as the ark got stolen, so was her life. She could not survive without God's glory.

As I was reading this account in the Bible, I was hit with waves of emotions. Tears began to stream down my face. I could hardly control my breathing. I felt the pain of this story as if I was there. Then, all of a sudden, I heard a question: What about the church? My heart sank.

The modern church has evolved and adapted to exist without the presence of God. She feels quite comfortable and content living without prayer, without experiencing the glory of God on a constant basis.

Not many tremble before His presence anymore. I see people playing on their phones as they take communion, oblivious to the moment's significance. I hear people evaluating the miraculous, labeling what they deem genuine or fake as if they are the experts on the Holy Spirit.

The first church used to pray and fast before ordaining someone to the ministry. These days, churches can ordain people so they don't leave elsewhere. The ministers used to be the men of prayer. Now, we assign men of stature and qualifications. We make Him move at our command because we run the schedule. The list can go on and on.

The Father is hurt seeing the Bride of His son totally unprepared. Many are redeemed but not radical in protecting Jesus amongst us.

SMOTHERING MOTHERS

Many believers act like the evil mother before King Solomon. This woman smothered her child while sleeping in the night. Realizing that she had killed her baby, she stole the roommate's child, claiming him as her own.

When they stood before the king, both claimed the same baby. Solomon commanded to cut the child into two. The woman who smothered her child shrugged impassively, "Let him be neither mine nor yours" (1 Kings 3:26, NKJV).

It hurts me even to write these words. Many church leaders do the same thing. They have "killed" the Son in their sleep. Yet, instead of pursuing God in repentance, they spend their energy killing the zeal in others.

If I have seen it once, I have seen it ten times. For example, the Holy Spirit begins to move through some youngsters. They start praying, seeking God. They start seeing healings, miracles, and the supernatural. And then the leaders show up.

Driven by jealousy that God is not moving through them the same way, they begin to control and rebuke the fire in those kids. I remember some teens being followed at night cause the church leaders needed to find out where they went to pray. What a job for the deacons—spiritual agents.

I have seen how some churches busied themselves with events, specifically on the days when revival services would be happening at other churches. I have seen how the leaders brought the moving of the Holy Spirit under their control, thus killing the move itself. After finding out that some of his people attended a large prayer meeting at another church, one pastor required his people to sign papers that they would not visit prayer meetings at other churches.

I have seen prayer groups wandering without a room to bend their knees. Every activity in the church building gets prioritized over prayer. Who cares about some mumbling elderly ladies? I have seen them pushed around from room to room and eventually from hallway to hallway. The pastor and the leaders are too busy to pray, but they won't let others do it either.

Not for me and not for you. Let Him be neither mine nor yours.

Under the same spirit of Saul, who grew jealous of David doing better than him, many church leaders bring down those that God is raising up. Instead of seeking God for themselves to move in the power too, they would rather kill the anointing doing what the woman wanted when she said, "Neither I nor you shall have him."

The orphan spirit is real. The syndrome of the older brother is real. Instead, we need more father and mother figures who can raise others to raise higher and go farther. Jesus had

> **If we are not careful, we will choke the life out of the Son.**

no issue saying that we would do greater works than Him (John 14:12).

If we are not careful, we will choke the life out of the Son in our lives, ministries, and churches. We must do everything possible to create the right spiritual environment so Jesus can feel welcomed, loved, and exalted.

TOLERATING JESUS

Just like Pharisees claimed Abraham was their father (John 8) while Jesus straightened them out by telling the devil is their father, so do many claim Jesus to be fully present in their midst when it's been decades since the last time He was welcomed.

When Jesus was hanging on the cross, the Pharisees kept playing the blame game. They mocked Jesus, "We want to believe in You. Of course, we do. Come down from the cross, perform a miracle for us, and we will believe. See, you don't want to do it. Maybe it is because you are not a God, or maybe it is because you don't want us to believe" (Matthew 27:42).

This wasn't the only time they spoke to Jesus this way. "Therefore they said to Him, 'What sign will You perform then, that we may see it and believe You? What work will You do?'" (John 6:30, NKJV).

Can you hear what the Pharisees actually said? They blamed Jesus for the fact that they did not believe in Him. They claimed they wanted to believe but without a need for faith. Make it make sense.

Similar stories can be heard from pulpits today. A particular pastor said, "I am not against healings and deliverances in our church. If God wants to come and heal someone, of course, I will not mind it."

It sounds so good and elevated, except for the fact that it is completely ignorant of the Word of God. First, who are we to not mind when God shows up? He owns us, not the other way around. Second, Jesus did not teach us to be tolerant of His gifts. Jesus told us to desire them eagerly (1 Corinthians 12:31). That's a big difference right there.

> But why do you call Me 'Lord, Lord,' and not do the things which I say? Whoever comes to Me, and hears My sayings and does them, I will show you whom he is like: He is like a man building a house, who dug deep and laid the foundation on the rock. And when the flood arose, the stream beat vehemently against that house, and could not shake it, for it was founded on the rock.
>
> **Luke 6:46–48 (NKJV)**

Jesus did not call us to be talkers and observers of His works. He called us to do His works and be intentional about everything Jesus did.

"And as you go, preach, saying, 'The kingdom of heaven is at hand.' Heal the sick, cleanse the lepers, raise the dead, cast out demons" (Matthew 10:7–8, NKJV).

JUDGING JESUS

What I described above is what Mario Murillo calls a Culture of Compromise in his *Edgewise* book. Many appear spiritual yet without the spirit to stand for the truth.

Taking an example from the 9/11 tragedy, Murillo writes, "9/11 exposed how incapable of outrage many in our nation are. After 3,000 innocent Americans were incinerated in the Twin Towers, many wanted to form committees to study 'what we did to make the terrorists mad.'"[60]

This is what the church does many times. Instead of celebrating heaven invading earth through the supernatural acts of healings, deliverances, and breakthroughs, the church summons meetings to evaluate and decide if those things are worth their seal of approval.

The modern church evaluates the Holy Spirit more than it values Him. The Holy Spirit is endlessly analyzed and not energized to make a difference. Many love the Holy Spirit in name but not in action.

Saul did something similar when God used his son, Jonathan, to provide a major victory against the Philistines (1 Samuel 14). Being an experienced warrior, Saul did a foolish thing. He put a curse on the army, forbidding them from eating.

> **Many appear spiritual yet without the spirit to stand for the truth."**

What a dumb declaration in the face of a fleeing enemy. What got into him?

This was an elementary mistake. Saul saw the fleeing enemy but did not chase after it to capitalize on the victory. He got stuck in internal political affairs. He should have strengthened the soldiers with the necessary provisions and gone after the Philistines.

And the reward to Jonathan for his faith and bravery? Death on the spot. Luckily, the lower-ranked soldiers had more sense to talk the king into mercy on his own son.

Paul Tripp writes, "When a pastor is responding to issues in his church in ways that are more political than pastoral, it's not because he's ignorant of the selfishness of this response but because he's more committed to building his kingdom than God's."[61]

We make similar mistakes at our leadership meetings. Sometimes, there need to be fewer meetings and more goings. There, I said it.

"Thus says Hezekiah: 'This day is a day of trouble, and rebuke, and blasphemy; for the children have come to birth, but there is no strength to bring them forth'" (2 Kings 19:3, NKJV).

The Lord gives ministries and the grace to be effective, but if the flesh finds its way, it will abort them. One of the prevailing symptoms of the flesh is the contradictions and irrational decisions of smart leaders in the church. Just like with Saul, the first part was amazing, with the Philistines taking a big hit, but the second part was totally foolish.

The modern church evaluates the Holy Spirit more than it values Him.

Some in ministry believe people can't change. This thought comes from much pain and discouragement, but it is contradictory. How can one be in the business of changing people's lives yet be convinced they don't change?

Jesus is still alive. His character can still be developed in people through the fruit of the Spirit. His ministry can still be effective through the gifts of the Spirit.

I want to challenge you—if people do not change in your ministry, do not seek some theological explanation that will excuse you to stay the same. Read the Bible and take God at His word. Do not settle until you see the lifestyle of Jesus represented in your life.

For several years now, I have been a part of a local prayer ministry. On the outside, this ministry has nothing attractive. We meet on the edge of our local Northwest civilization. It is located in a small town on the outskirts leading to the Columbia River Gorge.

People from many denominations gather in an almost century-old church building. During summer, the air conditioner often does not work, and of course, the heater does not work right during winter. There are no big speakers, worship bands, or cool decorations. The worship is played through a laptop while everyone prays, and an altar call is given after a short word.

These gatherings are filled with the supernatural. People get healed of chronic illnesses and diseases like cancer. Others get activated into ministry and start similar prayer meetings in other states.

There are countless deliverances taking place. Addictions to alcohol fall off. Depression and suicidal thoughts leave. The supernatural moves powerfully through words of knowledge, words of wisdom, and words of prophecy.

It is all done by regular Christians who do not hold any titles. They are regular believers who have regular jobs. The only difference is that they have decided to see God's promises come to pass no matter what.

This group of people also does night prayers every week. For over a decade now, people have prayed every Friday from midnight to six in the morning.

Usually, one would expect very spiritual people to be at such prayer meetings. But to my surprise, they are filled with teenagers and adults, many of whom come with personal issues. These people would not qualify for a Sunday church service ministry.

Some teenagers come to these night prayers and just sit or sleep through the night. I wondered why they even come if they are not praying. They are far away from being anything close to prayer warriors. So it seemed.

One guy, in particular, was seriously suicidal. He came to prayer because his friends dragged him in. I did not see his face for about two months because he always covered it with a hoodie. I never heard his voice because he was always silent.

But his life radically changed in just about two months as he was covered by prayer and the ministry of others. His testimony is powerful, and now he is on fire for Jesus. It all happened by coming to night prayers that he did not want to be a part of.

At these meetings, I have seen alcohol addictions fall, terrible back issues healed, suicidal thoughts broken off, how depression leaves and demonic torment ceases, prophetic insights given, and destiny uncovered.

Now, tell me that people do not change.

Cry out for the Son.

Robby Dawkins wrote in his book *Do What Jesus Did*, "When we walk in the presence and authority of God, we will do what Jesus did."[62]

Dawkins also wrote, "God's gift to us is ability; our gift to God is availability. He says to us, 'You go first. You be available and step out, and I will empower you in the moment.'"[63]

Dawkins summarized really well what I am writing about, "Somehow our 'religion' has made it too easy for us to forget the radically inclusive, table-turning, paradigm-shifting Christ of the Bible, and instead, subtly buy into the lie that Christianity is a little bit boring, a little bit old-fashioned and not quite true in the parts that count."[64]

A RADICAL TURN

Several years ago, when I first got activated in the prophetic, I had an exciting experience. My brother Vasiliy pastors a church in Sacramento, California, and invited me to speak.

During worship, I looked at one of the teens in the worship band playing a guitar and saw a prophetic impression. When it was my time to get up on stage and preach, I called the guy out and told him that I saw him at a fork in the road. One lane goes to the left and the other to the right.

It was not hard to understand the meaning. I said that he was at a decision point. He needs to decide which direction to go—left or right, this or that. I also reaffirmed that God will help him make the right decision.

As I relayed this, I noticed the young man getting slightly emotional. It must have meant something. I left it at that and moved on with my message.

The Lord orchestrated for me to be at my brother's church again in a few months when this teen named Erik was giving his life testimony.

As it turns out, Erik was backsliding. He followed his friends, smoking weed and partying. The peer pressure was great, and as a teen, Erik wanted to fit in.

Erik realized that he had to make a decision—friends or God. What shocked him the most was that God, who knew Erik was in the darkest part of his life, loved him enough to reach out to Erik while he was in sin. It rocked his world. He felt the Father's unconditional love at that moment, leading him to repentance. This is when Erik decided to dedicate his life to the Lord.

Currently, Erik is an ordained pastor, an anointed worship leader, and an evangelist preaching on the streets of Sacramento. What an amazing testimony of God's goodness. People do change. God is still on the move.

Let us not cheapen the Christian experience. It is glorious, and it is the best thing that can ever happen to a human being.

LOVESICK

We need Jesus. If you have Him, you need more. Never get satisfied with where you are. In the natural, when you eat or drink, you get quickly filled up. In the spiritual, the more you eat, the more hungry you get, and the more you drink, the more thirsty you get.

Be like Hannah, totally and utterly unsatisfied with the current state of the revelation of Jesus. Be like Rachel, crying out for Jesus as your life depends on it. Be like Eli's daughter-in-law, sensitive to the Spirit, recognizing when He comes and when He leaves. Be so closely attached to Him that life would lose meaning without His presence.

This is love. This is the heart of a true Bride who will not be distracted but ready for the Bridegroom.

> I opened for my beloved, But my beloved had turned away and was gone. My heart leaped up when he spoke. I sought

him, but I could not find him; I called him, but he gave me no answer.

The watchmen who went about the city found me. They struck me, they wounded me; The keepers of the walls Took my veil away from me.

I charge you, O daughters of Jerusalem, If you find my beloved, That you tell him I am lovesick!

Song of Solomon 5:6–8 (NKJV)

Let us be lovesick for the Lord. Let us go after Him, calling out His name in the night. Yes, the evil in this dark world will hurt and mistreat us. So be it. It is the price we are willing to pay as we chase after our Love.

And when you find Him, the Beloved will say, "O my love, you are as beautiful as Tirzah, Lovely as Jerusalem, Awesome as an army with banners! Turn your eyes away from me, For they have overcome me" (Song of Solomon 6:4–5, NKJV).

CHAPTER 11

TO THE CORRUPT CHURCH

IT IS CRITICALLY IMPORTANT TO GET IT RIGHT. The moment we lose the grip of eternity, we lose passion for His coming. We become earthly-minded, and Jesus' return becomes an undesirable event. The flesh deceives us and corrupts our vision.

I write praying that these truths will stir your heart to lose anything and everything of the flesh. I pray that God's Spirit inside of you would bubble up with jealousy and passion. To jealously crucify the flesh and to passionately pursue God's heart in purity.

Sometimes, we are simply not aware of the things that pile up. Even though we may be sincere, we can still be mistaken. But things can change as we open our hearts for repentance.

"For he who sows to his flesh will of the flesh reap corruption, but he who sows to the Spirit will of the Spirit reap everlasting life" (Galatians 6:8, NKJV).

Just like Eve relied on the flesh hoping for the Savior, so does modern Christianity, in many ways, rely on the flesh expecting spiritual results. Jesus said, "That which is born of the flesh is flesh, and that which is born of the Spirit is spirit" (John 3:6 NKJV)

We strive in the flesh to see spiritual results and wonder why it's not working. We quote the Bible verses, but they sound more irrelevant than ever because those declarations are not getting realized.

Regardless if you are a believer in Jesus, the acts of the flesh will still bring destruction and death. The flesh is sneaky, and it hides under a very spiritual facade. We must expose it to eliminate it and, once more, become a thriving body of Christ.

FLESHLY WORKS FOR SPIRITUAL RESULTS

I love the analogy R. T. Kendall draws in his book called *Pigeon Religion*. Kendall writes: "It is the encroachment of any teaching, ministry, or practice that you thought was a dove—the authentic Holy Spirit—but which turned out to be a pigeon—the counterfeit. In a word: the flesh, not the Spirit."[65]

In other words, some acts of the flesh present themselves very spiritually. Not everyone can recognize the fake representation of the dove—the Holy Spirit or the true teaching of the Bible.

When I write about the flesh, I do not mean your body. Your body is beautiful because God created it. The flesh is that part inside our souls that is carnal. Your body should be nourished and taken care of as the temple of God. The flesh, on the other hand, is something the Bible teaches us to kill and never let it arise. "Now those who belong to Christ Jesus have crucified the flesh with its passions and desires" (Galatians 5:24, NASB).

The flesh does have the power to resurrect if we are not careful. It knows how to put on a holy disguise. Let me list some ways it creeps into the Christian hearts and churches.

Drs. Jerry & Carol Robeson write, "Here are some works of the flesh that can spring up into full-blown problems: covetousness, envying, debate, strife, hatred, divisions, jealousy, and resentment. These are deadly seedlings that begin growing in our lives when we are not careful."[66]

"For to be carnally minded is death, but to be spiritually minded is life and peace" (Romans 8:6, NKJV).

Sometimes, we practice the flesh, hoping to see spiritual results. Other times, we practice spirituality to see fleshly results. We think that by applying all the spiritual principles, we will get the desired benefits on the horizontal plane.

I have been catching myself in this as well. As I write this, I am also repenting and letting the Holy Spirit do His work in my life. Here's how we try to apply spiritual works for the fleshly benefits.

For example, we tithe (a spiritual act) and immediately open our banking apps to see the hundred-fold reward. Oops, that didn't work. My money is out, and I did not get what I was promised. Flesh.

You cannot use God as an investment platform. He is not Wall Street.

"Honor the Lord with your possessions, And with the firstfruits of all your increase; So your barns will be filled with plenty, And your vats will overflow with new wine" (Proverbs 3:9–10, NKJV).

This Bible verse is amazing. It is quoted often during the offering calls. A preacher says something like, "Bring your offering and expect to be greatly blessed." That's what that Bible verse teaches. Yet, we skip the first part that starts with "honor the Lord." Tithing is not for getting rich but for honoring the Lord.

Some people tithe and declare they cannot get sick. But God is not a health insurance agency. It is not like He is collecting monthly premium payments and works to keep you healthy because of your works.

We are destined to live in divine health not because of what we do but because of what Jesus did when He put His back under the lashing whips for one reason—for us to be healthy (1 Peter 2:24).

I believe Jesus could have died in the garden of Gethsemane, and it would have been enough to justify us. He already bled there, and as we say, "His one drop is enough." Jesus was about to die, as He said in His own words, but He made up His mind to go all the way to ensure we are not only saved from sin but from every other curse on the earth that affected our bodies as well.

I would like to include an excerpt from the book by James Maloney called *The Dancing Hand of God*. Dr. Maloney clearly distinguishes between doing this for Christ versus doing things in Christ.

> Otherwise, many people base their sense of identity in ministry solely on what they're accomplishing for the Lord. They say, "Am I gaining acceptance before Him by doing this or that?" They also constantly strive in their lives to gain acceptance among their peers when they don't seemingly realize that everything they hope to achieve is found in ministering in the Person of Christ for the Lord Jesus Christ.
>
> If the apostles and apostolic people would enter into this key revelation, they would cease striving to gain acceptance and approval among peers, or from the Lord, for that matter. Now, I believe there is a place in ministry for acceptance, approval and honor—don't get me wrong. But many people allow it to be a driving force behind their ministries, so they're constantly frustrated because they can never seem to achieve that level of perfection that they envision their ministry expression should be at. And perhaps the initial vision of their ministry expectations was based on a faulty perception to begin with, because they thought it was what they could do for Christ, not what they could do in Christ.

MASKING IDOLATRY BEHIND BLESSINGS

James Maloney writes, "The apostles (I add "pastors and teachers") must teach the people of God the difference between the holy and the profane. Otherwise, we all attempt to minister out of our own shallowness and vanity, and we're not touching the people's spirits."[67]

We often quote Jesus when He said, "But seek first the kingdom of God and His righteousness, and all these things shall be added to you" (Matthew 6:33, NKJV). And so we come to church on Sunday and look for that thing that should have been already added to us. "God, I am seeking You. Where is the thing that I want? See? I showed up!"

One woman testified in her Instagram post, "I always sought the Lord first, and now I am finally in the season of getting everything that gets added." Great caption for a selfie in front of a new Mercedes.

I don't think this is what Jesus meant. It would make Him kind of cheap with poor taste in cars. I mean, if you will get something from God that is a rightful addition to your spirituality, why not go for a Lamborghini? Smirk.

Of course, God blesses us with many earthly things, but I do not think this is what He meant when He said, "All these things shall be added." How about if you seek first the kingdom of God, you will get Jesus, and then eternal life, and then direct access to the throne, and then your dedicated place in the heavenlies, and then your eternal reward, and a crown? On top of that, you receive freedom from oppression, sin, sickness, and all sorts of bondages here on the earth.

> As His divine power has given to us all things that pertain to life and godliness, through the knowledge of Him who called us by glory and virtue, by which have been given to us exceedingly great and precious promises, that through these you may be partakers of the divine nature, having escaped the corruption that is in the world through lust.
>
> **2 Peter 1:3–4 (NKJV)**

This is what you get by seeking the kingdom of God. It is the kingdom of a different realm. Just think about it. What is the most valuable thing in heaven? What about all the spiritual gifts? What about eternity and being able to approach the throne of God as an heir? These are the precious promises we get from seeking God first.

One of the biggest seductions of the flesh is the search for relevance. In his book called *Disappearing Church*, Mark Sayers draws several conclusions as to why the church in the West is shrinking.[68]

Seeking relevance corrupted the church in many ways, but deep reverence will restore her. Sayers analyzes, "The assumed belief was that people were uninterested in Christianity because they found church traditions and rituals alien and unwelcoming. If the church could be made relevant—with culturally relevant forms instead of traditions and ritualized trappings—the Christianity would flourish in the Western world again."[69]

The church wanted the world to like her; in return, she became unlikable to the Father.

Despite an enormous effort to modernize Christianity, Sayers observes that with "the contemporary church's decades-long quest for cultural relevance, it continues to struggle to gain ground in the secular West. The aging profile of the church inevitably means that many churches are demographically disappearing."[70]

The church wanted the world to like her; in return, she became unlikable to the Father.

> "It is a very ill omen to hear a wicked world clap its hands and shout 'well done' to the Christian man."
>
> **Charles Spurgeon**[71]

Jesus doesn't have to be relevant. The first church never tried to fit the mold. Instead of searching for the authenticity of the Holy Spirit that presents itself in signs, wonders, and miracles, the modern church looked for a way to blend in with the culture. This required a watered-down spin on God, Jesus, and the Holy Spirit.

SELF-DECEIT

Here is how we corrupt ourselves often. For example, we hear preaching that teaches about Joseph, who was an honest man, and so God made him a powerful leader. The preacher means that if you are honest, you will also become a great leader. It is just not true.

Oh no. Did someone already promise you a great position? I've often heard these cute phrases: "Everyone is a leader!" It sounds so satisfying to hear, but is it true?

If you look at the life of Joseph, his honesty only brought trouble and hardship. Joseph did not see any leadership in the future. His pure way of life was digging him a hole deeper and deeper.

The Bible says that Joseph even forgot the dreams he had when he was young. He remembered them only after seeing his brothers come and bow down to him. Well, that was an "aha" moment (Genesis 42:9).

The only reason why Joseph was a faithful man is because he wanted to please God. He answered to Potifar's wife, "How then could I do such a wicked thing and sin against God?" (Genesis 39:9, NIV). Joseph knew that even though his father and the rest of the family could not see him, God could. Many people died as martyrs because of their dedication to the faith, and they never became great leaders.

We hear sermons about Abraham that go something like this—Abraham gave tithes, and he was made rich. Abraham indeed gave tithes. Abraham was indeed wealthy. Yet, by putting these two sentences together, we get manipulation at its finest.

The preacher implies: give tithes, and you will also be rich. But Abraham did not give tithes to get rich. He was already pretty successful. Don't hide your eyes from looking at the root, at the "why." Abraham gave tithes to Melchizedek, by which he honored Jesus. There is zero indication that he wanted to get rich off his tithings (Hebrews 7:1–10).

See, we have made Christianity all about us. The Bible and Jesus are the means to finding success here on earth. They shouldn't be. Jesus is the sole goal. Everything that we are to do is to reach Him. We cannot misuse Jesus for our gain.

I have also heard sermons about Moses. He was humble, and God made him a great leader. It sounds true, but the implied meaning is, "Stay humble, and you will also become a great leader."

If you strive to be humble to become a great leader, you are already full of pride. Moses was truly humble. The last thing he wanted was to be a leader. Stop deceiving yourself. Look at the entire picture before drawing your conclusions. David Wilkerson said, "Faith comes by hearing all the Word, not just preferred sections."[72]

> **Pride always makes a humble impression.**

The Bible has to make sense in the light of the entire Word of God. Putting a verse into context does not mean reading a verse before and after your passage. Does your revelation align with the entire gamut of the Word written through all the books of the Bible? Don't worry; if it is a genuine revelation from God, you will never encounter contradictions.

Pride always makes a humble impression. And the flesh always makes a spiritual appeal.

Paul made it clear to the Romans, "For of Him and through Him and to Him are all things, to whom be glory forever" (Romans 11:36, NKJV). I don't want to use Jesus to fix my family issues. It is much more than that. I want to be proactive in my family to have a great relationship with my wife and kids because in the evening, I will go to pray, and I want to make sure the Father can hear me.

It is not so much Jesus for my family as it is my family for Jesus. I love Him so much that I cannot let an argument with my wife get in the way. I will admit I am wrong a hundred times because I do not want to be disconnected from God.

Jesus is not a magic wand to make things happen. Just ask the first church. Everything we do on this earth should be motivated by the loving desire to be closer to Him.

A SICK EXPERIENCE

When I was sick for over four years with a chronic illness, none of the promises of God seemed to be true in my life. Everything was in reverse. I wanted to die in my pain. The Bible verse that I often quoted during that season before Jesus healed me was Habakkuk 3:17–18 (NKJV):

> Though the fig tree may not blossom, Nor fruit be on the vines; Though the labor of the olive may fail, And the fields yield no food; Though the flock may be cut off from the fold, And there be no herd in the stalls—Yet I will rejoice in the Lord, I will joy in the God of my salvation.

What if He will not do something for you? At least for a season. Fleshly, Christianity cannot handle that. It wants everything now.

Wrong expectations lead to discouragement, and discouragement leads to backsliding. Let us get one thing straight—nothing on this earth should define us. Happiness cannot do it—Jesus was a man of sorrow. Success doesn't define us—the heroes of faith lived in the caves. God does not care about a pretty picture because there was nothing pretty about Jesus on the cross.

There is only one thing that defines us: Christ. We are rooted in Him. Our success is Jesus. Our righteousness is in His blood. It does not matter if someone is rich or poor. Christ defines everything.

But this prosperity Gospel creeps into the church, gradually shifting our faith into works. It causes us to believe that striving gets favor with the Lord.

Here is what I am trying to say:

I do not pray to reach God. I already have access to approach His throne in boldness (Hebrews 4:16).

I fast not to beg God out of desperation. This is not a hunger strike to get His attention. I am already more than enough in Him. I fast out of the desire to walk in tune with the Holy Spirit (2 Corinthians 9:8).

I tithe not to get rich. I am already a king and a priest with full authority over everything (Revelation 1:6).

I read the Bible not to ease my consciousness and feel cleaner or holier. My holiness is in His blood, not my works (John 1:7).

Can you see the difference here? You can do all the same things but with two different motives. Being rooted in the truth and not the flesh makes all the difference.

CHASING JESUS AND ELSE

We are all after Jesus, of course. The problem is when He is not the only thing we are after. Any extra addition to Jesus corrupts the church. Imagine if you had told your future spouse before getting married, "Honey, I will be 100 percent faithful to you and only to you 364 days a year. But one day a year, anything can happen." I don't think a wedding party would have happened anytime soon.

Or imagine if you would say to your future spouse, "You are my favorite one. There are other girls I like to hang out with, but you are the best for sure." No, not good.

If we dig deeper into this issue of the flesh, we may find the occult inspiration behind it. In *Larson's Book of Spiritual Warfare*, Bob Larson exposes the Human Potential Movement. He describes this demonic practice as "a system of salvation that depends on what we can do for ourselves, not what God's grace can accomplish by faith in the redemption of Christ. The movement is humanistic, with humanity at the center of its hope to avoid fear and failure instead of centering on the help of the Holy Spirit." [73]

Recently, I met a person who shared a deep issue with me. He needed a resolution. I asked him if he tried praying about it. He stared at me like a deer staring at the headlights.

He said he wanted practical help. He wanted something tangible. It did not even cross his mind that he could have simply prayed about it to the living God. Why? Because he always consumed self-centered, self-motivational messages. He begged me to uncover a solution within himself.

Prayer is practical.

Humanistic preaching eliminated a prayer as anything real. Instead, it becomes easier to receive some steps to follow, some tasks to complete, and some work to do, so the reward is more justified. And if not, you can point to heaven and say, "Well, I tried."

This person's eyes told me, "What do you mean by asking me to pray? Are you kidding me? I come to you for practical help and not something abstract! Give me something tangible, something a bit more strategic and real."

Prayer is practical.

One of the most popular phrases in the culture that had weaved its way into the church is, "Follow your heart!" It's such a beautiful and inspirational slogan. One might even think it's biblical because the Bible says that God shall give us the desires of our hearts (Psalm 37:4).

Yet, the first part of the verse is often overlooked. It tells us first to learn to delight ourselves in the Lord. While many preach, teach, declare, and follow the desires of their hearts, the Bible states, "Cursed is the man who trusts in man And makes flesh his strength…" (Jeremiah 17:5, NKJV).

Let me make it blunt for you. You are a man. Putting trust in yourself and following your heart can be the very thing that leads you to corruption.

Who can know the heart of man? "The heart is deceitful above all things, And desperately wicked" (Jeremiah 17:9, NKJV). This is why we must be like David, pleading with God to "Search me, O God, and know my heart; Try me, and know my anxieties; And see if there is any wicked way in me, And lead me in the way everlasting" (Psalm 139:23-24, NKJV).

Jesus is the way, the truth, and the life. We are not going anywhere good if it is not in Him. Jesus is everything and is the greatest thing we can ever need or want.

Interestingly, the Old Testament temple had three entrances leading from the outside and all the way to the Holy of Holies. The first entrance was called The Way. The second one was called The Truth. The third one was called, you guessed it, The Life.[74]

When the Israelites heard Jesus say this phrase, they understood it differently than we do. The claim was by far more presumptuous. Jesus declared that He is the true temple, the presence of God, and the embodiment of the law.

Dr. J. Vernon McGee writes, "The only possible alternative is for him to get on the right way or be utterly wrong. 'I am the way...' In making this tremendous claim, He repudiated every other way. The way into God's presence, the place of communion and worship, is through Christ."[75]

It is all spiritual, yet we try to manipulate it into a self-gaining justification. Just quit it. You must learn to discern when the Word is used and abused for egoistic reasons and not for drawing nearer to God.

HUMANISTIC FAITH

"By catering our worship to the worshippers and not to the Object of our worship, I fear we have created human-centered churches," writes Francis Chan.[76] This is a terrible reality.

No Christian will openly agree that Jesus is not the way, the truth, or the life. Yet, when it comes to being practical, we often rely on essential human experience more than Jesus. Those things are logic, philosophy, and, many times, psychology. The modern church is guilty of humanism.

The church leans on philosophy and psychology like the first church leaned on the gifts of the Holy Spirit. I remember when the Steve Jobs' book came out. Pastors would quote Jobs' wisdom and strategies at every leader's meeting and even at some of the sermons. It always made me cringe, as if the Bible cannot teach strategy.

Now, so many believers chat excitedly about the latest interviews with Andrew Tate and how he shares so much truth and wisdom into the lives of young men. I cringe again, as if there is no godly example to follow, reserving to a millionaire who converted from Christianity to Islam and made his fortune in the porn industry.

Many Christians can better quote business books and follow more celebrities on social media than knowing the Bible and being inspired by the true men of God. The strong men of this world can say good things, but they are often sprinkled with all sorts of garbage simultaneously. It would be exhausting to pick it all apart.

Derek Prince wrote, "Beware when people start to use a lot of psychological jargon and invoke the support of psychiatrists for the truth of the gospel. The gospel doesn't need the support of psychiatrists... The Bible stands without the endorsement of psychiatrists or philosophers or scientists or anybody."[77]

The Gospel is quite simple, and it is highly effective when kept that way.

- How can I grow spiritually? The cross.
- How can I be holy? Jesus.
- How can I love my wife better? The cross.
- How can my family be stronger? Jesus.
- I don't know what to do with my life. Lay it down on the cross.
- How can I get my prayers answered? Jesus.
- I deal with so much fear. You need Jesus.

Kenneth Hagin taught, "We must have this spirit of wisdom and revelation of Christ and His Word if we are to grow. It is not going to be imparted to us through our intellect, either. The Holy Spirit must unveil it to us."[78]

Jesus is the fulness of the Gospel. You will not find anything wiser than Jesus. There is nothing more profound than Jesus. There is no other way but Jesus. You will not find anything lighter to carry than the cross or anything more precious than the cross. You will not find a better partner than the Holy Spirit or experience a greater power than the Holy Spirit.

These days, even many salvations are done in the flesh. This is why many people accept Jesus, yet their spiritually newborn enthusiasm is nearly zero. They still show up to church only once a month. They are still not interested in prayer meetings. I used to be puzzled by this. Why?!

It is because we manipulate people into Christianity. For example, I have been to services when the preacher would say, "Now every head bowed, and every eye closed. No one looks around. It is between you and God. Raise your hand if you want to accept Jesus." People raise their hands, and the pastor says, "Now, everyone who raised their hands, come forward."

My question is, why did you ask them to close their eyes in the first place? Why did you say to everyone not to look around? You set those poor people up.

At the end of his message, this other evangelist once said, "If you want the fire of God, come forward to the altar." Many in the church came forward. Who wouldn't want the fire of God? And so this evangelist prays, "Thank you, Jesus, for all these people that came forward to accept you as their Savior."

That's one way to drive salvation counts up for reporting purposes. And we wonder why this whole thing does not have a lasting effect.

Sadly, not much has changed since almost seventy years ago when Leonard Ravenhill wrote his book *Why Revival Tarries*. He wrote, "The evangelists today are very often prepared to be anything to anybody as long as they can get somebody to the altar for something. They glibly call out: 'Who wants help? Who wants more power?" Who wants a closer walk with God?' Such a sinning, repenting 'easy believism' dishonors the blood and prostitutes the altar."[79]

Some teach how to lead people best to accept God. In one particular video lesson, a pastor stressed the fact that most of the people in the United States live just fine. They don't have crazy struggles. This is why your altar call needs to go something like this, "You may have a good life, but there is a better life."

> **The Holy Spirit is your best partner and your greatest power.**

This is an altar call that hits on the flesh so well, appealing to selfishness and greed. Leonard Ravenhill writes, "We must alter the altar, for the altar is a place to die on. Let those who will not pay this price leave it alone!"[80]

Jesus did not die to give us a better life on earth. He came to redeem us. The first church did not have many earthly benefits. In fact, they lost them all. But what they gained was so precious that it was worth the exchange.

The prayers for repentance nowadays are also different. They mention that we accept Jesus, but the part that is often overlooked is, "Lord, I admit that I am a sinner. Forgive me." And so people accept Jesus like yet another God. They don't fully know what they are doing. They accept Jesus without acknowledging what He is doing for them.

The first word of the Gospel is "Repent!" When John the Baptist started his ministry, he cried out, "Repent for the kingdom of God is at hand!" (Matthew 3:2). When Jesus began His ministry, He started with the same phrase (Matthew 4:17). It was the same call with the disciples (Matthew 10:17).

Revival is coming. I can see it in my spirit. I can see the revival flooding our nation like a tsunami. This revival will be like a flood that covers all the states and all the cities. It will fill all the streets and neighborhoods. The coming revival will invade and saturate the entire nation and spill into the rest of the world.

But it will not come without real repentance and renewal. Let us turn our faces towards Christ again. He is Spirit, and He is looking for those who will live by the Spirit. We were born of the Spirit, and Galatians 5:25 (NKJV) says, "If we live in the Spirit, let us also walk in the Spirit."

PROPHETIC PLAGIARISM

Speaking of the corrupted church, I cannot ignore this one. Some go to such extremes as to borrow and declare the prophetic words of others. They do not always say that the Lord had specifically revealed it to them, but the assumption in the congregation is that.

"In a frenzy to stay popular some will steal the revelation of other preachers and claim them as their own," writes Mario Murillo.[81] It's one thing to steal the revelations of the Bible. I'd say that, in a way, we all borrow and feed from the same source. Paul would probably not mind that we quote and expound his writings often.

Yet, this plagiarism I am writing about goes to another level when preachers steal prophetic words and present them as their own. For example, one respectable minister prophesied that Trump would be president for the second term, and many jumped on that bandwagon without getting that revelation for themselves directly from God. They decided to ride on someone else's revelation and failed.

Others seek out prophetic words from different gifted people looking for something they can deliver during a service later on. Instead of cultivating an intimacy with the Holy Spirit on their own, they rather chase a gift in another man.

This is why Jeremiah 23:30 (NKJV) says, "Therefore behold, I am against the prophets', says the Lord, 'who steal My words every one from his neighbor."

Mimicking the prophetic reminds me of the sons of Sceva, who copied the apostle Paul without actually knowing God the way the apostle Paul did (Acts 19). Dangerous. Instead of seeking God and hearing Him for themselves, they imitated Paul.

In the end, the result is the same as with the sons of Sceva. If you rush into ministry without Jesus, you will be crushed by the mischief of the devil.

> **If you rush into ministry without Jesus, you will be crushed by the mischief of the devil.**

Look, Paul was happy even when the Gospel was shared for impure motives. "What then? Only that in every way, whether in pretense or in truth, Christ is preached; and in this I rejoice, yes, and will rejoice" (Philippians 1:18, NKJV). The Word of God will do its job in the hearts of the listeners, but it may still harm deeply the one who preaches.

Shawn Bolz writes about the prophetic, "He (God) wants to break through our manipulative ways, in which we use natural and spiritual information to get ahead, to help us get out of a performance mentality."[82] The phrase "fake it 'til you make it" should never apply to prophetic gifts.

This can seem permissible or perhaps even innocent in some situations. After all, people raise their hands and get touched. But this is what James Maloney would call in his *The Dancing Hand of God*, (Volume 2) book—The Balaam Spirit.

In short, the Balaam Spirit is the imitation of the divine. This was happening to Balaam because of his love for material gain.[83] It is one thing when someone passes down a word for you to deliver and another thing to claim it as your own. Spiritual plagiarism.

Why don't you lock yourself in the closet and seek God until you can hear His voice for yourself? He wants to talk to you personally. He is not mad at you, and you are not a second-class believer. Have faith, and don't settle for anything less but a direct and close relationship with the Holy Spirit.

None of us are immune from this problem. Even the prophet Nathan fell for it when he prophetically reassured King David he could go ahead and start building the biggest church building of that era. The prophet Nathan said, "Nathan said to the king, "Go, do all that is in your heart, for the Lord is with you" (2 Samuel 7:3, NKJV).

Nathan was a true prophet, but in this case, he was wrong. Why would he say that? I believe Nathan studied under the prophet Samuel and heard what Samuel told Saul when Saul was becoming a king (1 Samuel 10:7). Nathan prophesied to David the words that Samuel gave to Saul.

We can learn here that the same prophetic word to one person does not mean it always can apply to another. It was a mistake on behalf of Nathan. God did not strike him dead but simply woke him up that night to return to David and correct himself. Nathan was humble to do it, and what followed was an amazing prophecy that came to pass.

Nathan would have been better off talking to God before answering and not using other people's prophetic words. (You can find the whole story in 1 Chronicles 17.)

Let's repent of our fleshly ways. Let's come back to the Spirit. Let's come back to Christ. Divorce your flesh. In fact, crucify it. Please examine your heart and ensure you are not a church corrupted by the flesh. Purify yourself to be a ready Bride that had stood strong in the face of the great worldly temptations.

READY OR NOT

CHAPTER 12

THE BEGINNING OF THE END

"... Those who behold His sign know that the time of His appearing draws near. 'The wise shall understand.' (Daniel 12:10) and, like the Magi, they shall 'rejoice with great joy,' and follow it over a lonely, hazardous way, through hardships, heartaches and delay until, at last, they too shall come to a 'house' (a greater house built of 'living stones'), and to a 'child'—the man child..."[84]

James Maloney. *Ladies of God*. Volume 1

A FEW MONTHS INTO WRITING THIS BOOK, I had two consecutive dreams on the same night. It was almost as if the Holy Spirit was speaking the same way as in Joseph's life. "And the dream was repeated to Pharaoh twice because God establishes the thing, and God will shortly bring it to pass" (Genesis 41:32, NKJV).

In my first dream, a particular pastor invited me to his church for a meeting. We met and proceeded into the meeting room when

I arrived at the building. Suddenly, the Holy Spirit takes me out of the building. I am rushed through the air and lowered onto the sidewalk opposite that church building.

Then, in front of my eyes, the entire building collapses. It was a brick structure, but now, not one brick is laid on another. The entire building was crumbled down. The scene was scary, and I understood such destruction is irreversible.

Immediately after this dream, I had another. In this dream, what I understood to be the Holy Spirit was a person sitting in a church office behind the pastor's desk. He called the pastor in to inform him of the verdict on his ministry.

I was allowed by that person (the Holy Spirit) to observe the situation, almost like a witness. I saw the Holy Spirit writing things on pages of documents. He was silent and serious. With a pen in His hands, He kept signing different parts of the paper.

The pastor who was called up was in panic mode. He was shaking. He paced around the office and even choked on his coffee, drinking it nervously. This pastor tried to talk to the person behind his desk but was immediately interrupted, "I was your friend. We knew each other well, but I am a judge right now. This is not a joke. You had your chance, and now there is no going back on this."

I looked closer into the paper that the Holy Spirit was signing. He was legally stripping that pastor off of his title. That pastor was demoted of his spiritual stature.

I woke up with a sense of fear and worry. This was serious. It was not just a dream; ignoring it would be unwise.

I asked the Holy Spirit, "What do I do with this? This is too serious to talk about. I can't just go around and preach it. You need to confirm this word, so I know I am speaking a true prophetic revelation." Within a week, the Holy Spirit verified this dream was from Him at least on four separate occasions.

Mario Murillo warns, "Two things would shock us to our core: if we knew our true condition before God, and if we knew how close America is to destruction. We need a Godsend."[85]

We are living as in the days of Noah (Matthew 24:37). Not only the modern culture but the church has also been largely intruded by the enemy. Derek Prince listed the prominent issues that led to the flood, "Number one, satanic infiltration. Number two, corrupted thought life. Number three, sexual perversion. Number four, violence. Number five, blatant, aggressive homosexuality. Number six, materialism. And number seven, the good thing one man who walked with God."[86]

> **Jesus declares a coming punishment while looking for our discernment and humbleness to revert it.**

The reason why the judgment will begin at the house of God first (1 Peter 4:17) is that the things listed above have penetrated the modern church. We are living in the days of Noah.

God pronounces judgment for the sake of repentance. Jesus declares a coming punishment while looking for our discernment and humbleness to revert it. He says He will do it but hopes it won't be necessary.

"The Lord is not slack concerning His promise, as some count slackness, but is longsuffering toward us, not willing that any should perish but that all should come to repentance" (2 Peter 3:9, NKJV).

I understand this can sound harsh and hard to receive. But trust me, this is nothing yet. The apostle Paul writes, "Knowing, therefore, the terror of the Lord, we persuade men" (2 Corinthians 5:11, NKJV). Do any of us know the terror of the Lord? How often do we preach or hear sermons from this perspective? The modern church has yet to meet this kind of Jesus—"He was clothed with a robe dipped in blood, and His name is called The Word of God" (Revelation 19:13, NKJV).

He is the Word of God that cuts through to the division of soul and spirit, joints and marrow, and is a discerner of the thoughts and intents of the heart (Hebrews 4:12). When was the last time you experienced such piercing?

God will never put people up against the wall without a way out. Even at His harshest, He will show a way out if one is willing to take it. Jesus told the Laodicean church He would spit them out while instructing them how to avoid it.

The Holy Spirit speaks to the modern church—"Repent and ready yourself. Be willing to change, and the wrath will be reverted." Mark Sayers writes in his *Reappearing Church* book, "For renewal to come, we must first reach the point where we make a choice to no longer tolerate our current state of being."[87] "Nevertheless, when the Son of Man comes, will He really find faith on the earth?" (Luke 18:8, NKJV).

As you have read through the book, were there any areas in your life worth talking to Jesus about? Is there complacency in your life or ministry? Was it a long time since you have seriously considered His second coming? Are you driven by eternity or by blessings in this life? Be vulnerable with yourself and the Holy Spirit right now. It's between you and Him. Pause reading and talk to Him a little. Soften your heart so that He can do a beautiful work in you.

END-TIME BIRTH PAINS

From the very beginning of human history, people of faith lived in great anticipation of the Savior. Those who were ignorant were impassionate about God. From Eve in Genesis to John in Revelation, we are inspired again and again to long for the coming of Christ. Now, in the twenty-first century, we are reaching the resolution of all things. We are on the verge of the appearance of the Son of Man.

It won't be long before we will see Jesus face to face. We will see as John saw, "Then I, John, saw the holy city, New Jerusalem, coming down out of heaven from God, prepared as a bride adorned for her husband" (Revelation 21:2, NKJV).

Very soon, the angel will proclaim, "Come, I will show you the bride, the Lamb's wife" (Revelation 21:9, NKJV). At the end of the book, the angel calls her a wife. She will be ready, and she will get married. That's a promise.

The Father has the second coming on schedule, but not even His Son has received the calendar invite. "But of that day and hour no one knows, not even the angels of heaven, but My Father only" (Matthew 24:36, NKJV).

For Jesus, it will be a sudden event, just like for us. Life in eternity will go on in its perfect beat when the Father approaches Jesus and says, "Son, it is time. You may go to your Bride now." At that moment, even Jesus must be ready to make His descent quickly. He won't get an advanced notice.

The Father is keeping this grandest secret in the entire universe all to Himself, but He did not leave us without a clue. This is why I write about it confidently. Though we do not know the day and the hour, we know exactly in what season. Jesus gives us five points defining the season in which He will return.

1. Deception will run rampant (Matthew 24:4; 10–12)
We covered this throughout the book. Countless people are fooled into all sorts of counterfeit Jesuses, fake salvations, and wide roads into heaven. More and more churches and denominations are moving away from sound doctrine. Take even the last ten years as an example; lawlessness is on a continuous rise.

2. Wars and rumors of wars (Matthew 24:6)
Unlike at any time in human history, wars are everywhere. They are happening more and more frequently all over the world. This is unprecedented. A hundred years ago, we even had to come up with a new term that never existed before—a world war.

3. Natural disasters (Matthew 24:7)

Terrible earthquakes, epidemics, and famines are taking place all over the world now as well. The record of earthquakes is more and more frequent each year. There are more starving people than at any point in history, even though we have more food than at any point in history.

4. Persecution of Christians (Matthew 24:9)

Today, we also have the most persecuted Christians than at any other point in history. It may seem otherwise living in America, but it is not so on a global scale. Even in the US, the hostility towards Christianity rises quickly.

5. The Gospel reaching the entire world (Matthew 24:14)

The fifth clue is the only good one. It is also true today that while the darkness is at its worst, God's light is shining at its brightest. People accept Jesus in multitudes unlike ever before in history. The Gospel covers the globe, leaving only a few spots that are not yet reached.

Jesus said in indignation, "Hypocrites! You can discern the face of the sky and of the earth, but how is it you do not discern this time?" (Luke 12:56, NKJV). We cannot be ignorant. Recognize the times we are living in and start acting accordingly. If not, the same will happen as with Jerusalem when Jesus cried, regretting that the people did not know the time of His visitation (Luke 19:41–44).

Jesus gave us a lot of clues. We do not have a single excuse for not recognizing that these are the last days we are living in.

The five signs are what Jesus described as "the beginning of birth pains" (Matthew 24:8, NIV). There is no way to prevent those things from happening. They must take place for Jesus to appear. The pains must begin in order for a Child to be born.

"For you yourselves know perfectly that the day of the Lord so comes as a thief in the night. For when they say, 'Peace and safety!' then sudden destruction comes upon them, as labor pains upon a pregnant woman. And they shall not escape" (1 Thessalonians 5:2–3, NKJV).

If you had a pregnant wife about to deliver a baby, you'd notice her in terrible pain. It would be foolish of you to call the doctor and beg him to stop that. Every grown person understands that the mother must endure pain to deliver the joy of her life.

Many believers today pray for all those labor symptoms to stop, not realizing they are praying against the second coming of the Bridegroom. The first church never prayed for the persecution to end. They asked for boldness instead (Acts 4:29). We also must pray the same prayer as we live through these pains. Aren't we excited to finally receive the Son?

But how do we get ready?

FIRST, BE TOTALLY COMMITTED TO JESUS

This is a heart relationship that is not based on religion or doctrine. It is not an intellectual connection. This whole-hearted approach is completely, fully, and totally surrendered to Him.

This devoted relationship leaves no room for the flesh. There are no secondary lovers. There is only one thing, one man, one devotion, one love—Jesus Christ the Bridegroom. "For 'the two,' He says, 'shall become one flesh.' But he who is joined to the Lord is one spirit with Him" (1 Corinthians 6:16–17, NKJV).

Being joined with the Lord and becoming one spirit with Him means acting, thinking, and living like Him. "'For this reason a man shall leave his father and mother and be joined to his wife, and the two shall become one flesh.' This is a great mystery, but I speak concerning Christ and the church" (Ephesians 5:31–32, NKJV).

This is a big deal. Of course, we all understand in part and interpret in part. Even the apostle Paul had to pause and confess that being one with Jesus is a great mystery. To make better sense of this, Paul used the relationship between a husband and a wife as an example of the relationship the Bride needs to have with Jesus.

We must do our part as Jesus has already done His part by which we got engaged to Him. "For I am jealous for you with Godly jealousy, for I have betrothed you to one husband that I may present you as a chaste virgin to Christ" (2 Corinthians 11:2, NKJV).

Betrothed means that it is much more serious than an engagement. It cannot be broken. If it does, it is treated as adultery and divorce.

> Do you not know that the unrighteous will not inherit the kingdom of God? Do not be deceived. Neither fornicators, nor idolaters, nor adulterers, nor homosexuals, nor sodomites, nor thieves, nor covetous, nor drunkards, nor revilers, nor extortioners will inherit the kingdom of God. And such were some of you...
> **1 Corinthians 6:9–11 (NKJV)**

We are reminded of our past and where God positioned us now by His grace. The apostle Paul does not shy away by saying, "Such were some of you" (1 Corinthians 6:11, NKJV). Yet, by preaching the Gospel, Paul brought salvation to the Corinthians. In this process, he engaged them to Jesus Christ.

Then, Paul writes, "But I fear, lest somehow, as the serpent deceived Eve by his craftiness, so your minds may be corrupted from the simplicity that is in Christ" (2 Corinthians 11:3, NKJV). The word "simplicity" Paul used in Greek means two things—simplicity and sincerity.

So, even though it was a real engagement, it was legitimate, yet Paul feared it might have all been annulled.

Some say we cannot lose our salvation because it is a gift, and God will not take His gift back. Maybe He won't, but you can always throw it away. We cannot apply human logic to spiritual reality. Some say that if you have backslidden, you have never been truly saved. But we read above that it was all genuine. They were saved. They were engaged, but by craftiness, they got deceived.

The church got tricked by basic things, really. Simplicity and sincerity. Paul could not have said it any better. These two things are probably the rarest gems on earth right now. Especially here in the USA, we have forgotten how to live simply.

We are all about upgrades, making it better and better, as long as the payment can be handled. No one asks for the final cost; just show the monthly cost, and it's good. So crafty.

Nothing is wrong with upgrades when the Lord blesses you. But there is craftiness of the enemy we need to watch out for. When you try to fit in with the standards of your peers and match their lifestyle, your mind can quickly get occupied by worldly things, leaving you robbed from setting your mind on the things above (Colossians 3:2).

> **We cannot plug human logic into spiritual reality**

You may want something so badly that you are willing to take a second job or decide to work extra hours to handle the payments for what you are getting. Nothing is sinful here, but it takes away the time, energy, and zeal that could have been invested in the relationship with the Bridegroom.

I am not against blessings. I will upgrade to a better house whenever the Lord blesses me. But I will not stress or strive about the things that will burn away. I want to be devoted to my Bridegroom.

And sincerity. It is scarce. Not many are truly honest these days. Things are always sugarcoated. Everyone is overly nice, but I'd rather hear what you truly believe. Convict me when necessary.

After all, the Bible encourages us to speak to each other about our mistakes. How can it be done without sincerity? "Grace be with all those who love our Lord Jesus Christ in sincerity" (Ephesians 6:24, NKJV).

The lack of these two simple things can lead us astray so far that it can cause our engagement to fall out.

"So Christ was offered once to bear the sins of many; to those who eagerly wait for Him He will appear a second time apart from sin for salvation" (Hebrews 9:28, NKJV).

To whom will He appear? To those who eagerly wait for Him. Those who are in great expectancy. Just like the heroes of the Old Testament. Just like the first church. He will not appear to others for salvation when He comes back. It will be too late. He will come for a different group of people.

The Bride's first concern is to be ready for the Bridegroom's return, eagerly awaiting Him.

So, let me ask you, are you desiring? Are you longing for the return of the Bridegroom? Are you eagerly waiting, not just waiting, but eagerly waiting? Do you want His return, or does the end-times message scare you? Some say, "No, Lord, don't come just yet. There is still so much to do."

How can you pray that? Did you ever pray like this about your future spouse? "Hey, girl, I want to get married to you. We are already engaged. But I don't want to set the date 'cause I don't know when I will be done having fun with my single friends." Good luck with that wedding.

Don't tell Jesus you love Him if you don't want Him to come. A Bride's heart is on alert 24/7, expecting His arrival. No slack, no vanity. She is waiting, and she will not be distracted.

SECOND, GET APPROPRIATE CLOTHING

The second thing that is needed is the proper clothing. The Bible talks a lot about clothes, especially in Revelation.

> And I heard, as it were, the voice of a great multitude, as the sound of many waters and as the sound of mighty thunderings, saying, "Alleluia! For the Lord God Omnipotent reigns! Let us be glad and rejoice and give Him glory, for the marriage

of the Lamb has come, and His wife has made herself ready." And to her it was granted to be arrayed in fine linen, clean and bright, for the fine linen is the righteous acts of the saints.

Revelation 19:6–8 (NKJV)

Derek Prince taught, "When we first receive Jesus by faith as Savior and Lord, His righteousness is imputed to us. But as we live for Him, it has to be outworked in our lives. And what this is talking about is not imputed righteousness but outworked righteousness. Her bridal dress is made up of righteous acts."[88]

The Bride's wedding dress is knitted from her righteous acts. This is not to mistake the righteousness received at the moment of salvation, which is free. It is received at the altar. The righteous acts are something else.

Some argue we don't need to work because we have received salvation by faith, not by works. That is correct, but righteousness works. Righteousness has a lifestyle.

We are not saved by works, but saved people work.

The church still has a lot of work to do to prepare herself. I love how Derek Prince put it: "I've permitted myself to say sometimes, according to my observation, the contemporary church has got just about enough material to make a bikini. But that's not suitable for a marriage."[89]

"Behold, I am coming as a thief. Blessed is he who watches, and keeps his garments, lest he walk naked and they see his shame" (Revelation 16:15, NKJV).

We have to start preparing now. No bride begins this process when the bridegroom comes. The bride prepares beforehand; tomorrow is too late if you are not doing that now. Don't plan to start preparing later. That is when He will come. You must be ready now.

In the messages to the seven churches (Revelation 2 and 3), there is one thing that Jesus says to every church. "I know your works. I know what you're doing." Jesus does not say, "I know your doctrinal statement, your denominational statements, your theological background."

In other words, Jesus says, "I don't really need to hear your words. I know your works." Are your works righteous? The believers have received righteousness, but many do not act accordingly.

Many accept Jesus and get a little better. They repent and say that they quit smoking. Great, you should have not been smoking in the first place. Others say that they stopped yelling at their spouses. Great, you should have not been doing that in the first place.

I want to see those repentances again when people used to turn around one hundred and eighty degrees: repentances that set people on fire, causing them to show up for every prayer meeting and every gathering of the saints, making them burn with the commission of Christ.

If there is no prayer meeting, they will start one. They become devoted to the Word. They fall in love with Jesus because they know what has been exchanged for their righteousness.

Now, we see people repent, and the only noticeable difference is that you may see them a little more often on Sundays. When they come, they hang out in the hallway during the service, but hey, at least they're at church, right?

I see people repent and get baptized just so the pastor could have the legal or moral right to officiate their wedding. Once that is done, they are gone with the wind. The couple knew what they were doing. The pastor knew what they were doing. Yet, none of them had any fear of the Lord enough to do what was right. This attitude towards the most sacred spiritual acts would not pass by lightly in the first church.

"But when he saw many of the Pharisees and Sadducees coming to his baptism, he said to them, 'Brood of vipers! Who warned you to flee from the wrath to come? Therefore bear fruits worthy of repentance'" (Matthew 3:7–8, NKJV).

By today's standards, John was out of line. I mean, come on. Those poor Pharisees wanted to get baptized. Why would he do them like that? That was so rude. I'm being sarcastic if you haven't noticed.

John knew the hearts of those Pharisees and Sadducees were not right. He saw them through. Getting baptized could have gotten them a better standing with the enormous crowds gathering around John. Maybe this would even help the Pharisees to get into the inner circle with John's followers. Their baptism was a religious act, not a relational commitment.

There was no man-pleasing found in John the Baptist. He told the religious leaders they couldn't escape judgment just by getting wet. Their lifestyle had to prove that repentance was genuine. Dr. Randy Clark said in his sermon, "I believe across America there are hundreds of thousands of people sitting in our pews and think they are saved, and they're not."[90] Clark adds that a part of that reason is the leaders' fault who do not hold a high standard for what it means to be born again.

> **You are not saved by repeating a prayer but by rearranging your way.**

In Greek, the term for repentance means "to change your mind and amend your ways." You are not saved by repeating a prayer but by rearranging your way to forsake what is wrong.

Where is the fear of the Lord? Many so-called believers are lucky the proximity of the Holy Spirit is not as it was in the book of Acts when even lying had different consequences (Acts 5). As believers, especially ministers, we must have a higher moral standard.

Mark Sayers wrote, "God's whole business is renewal. When we engage in it, we follow His ways."[91] Many Christians live like Jesus, but before He turned thirty. They are good, God-fearing people but without the power of the Holy Spirit.

When Jesus said, "The works that I do you will do also and even greater works" (John 14:12). He did not mean that you would make more money than Jesus did working for His dad. He did not mean you would build a better business than He did before going into ministry.

Speaking of the greater works, Jesus meant the three-and-a-half-year period when He walked in the power of the Holy Spirit. When He delivered, saved, and healed, this is what He was calling to.

I am not trying to judge anyone. Please understand me. Do you realize what the Lord has done for us? He gave us eternity, and He gave us power, but in return, many give Him passivity. God so loved the world that He gave His only begotten Son. He has done this for us, but in return, we don't even want to give up our bad habits. As a church, we need to fall in love with God anew.

I do not want to be simply a saved person. I want to be the Bride of Christ. I have a vision for my life. I have a goal to marry Him one day. This vision helps me to fight the flesh. Doing that is so much easier when you want to be the Bride. It is so much easier to serve and minister when I know that I knit my wedding garment with every act of righteousness.

Kim Clement used to sing a prophetic song in his meetings. He sang gently something like this: "Sacrifice is beautiful; I'm in love with you. Sacrifice is easy; I'm in love with you."

All the believers will make it to the wedding feast, but I want to be the one who is getting married. I don't want to be an observant or a guest. I want to sit at the Bridegroom's table. I want to be the one beside Jesus' heart.

I don't want to be the one who barely made it so far out there from the Bridegroom that only His silhouette is noticeable. No, I want to hear Him breathing. I want to be so close to Him that a whisper would be enough to hear His voice clearly.

Do you have a record of your righteous acts? The things you do for the Lord will become the dress you will wear. We will be clothed in what we have done for the Lord. If you want to be the Bride of Christ who waits for His coming, be proactive. Do not wait for the right emotions. Get out there and start working on your wedding attire.

THIRD, STAY ALERT

The third and final step is critically important. It holds the first two together. This is something Jesus talked about repeatedly whenever He addressed the end times. Jesus instructed the early believers to never let go of this one single matter. Here are some mentions.

- "***Watch*** therefore, for you do not know what hour your Lord is coming" (Matthew 24:42, NKJV).
- "Therefore you also ***be ready***, for the Son of Man is coming at an hour you do not expect" (Matthew 24:44, NKJV).
- "So you also, when you see all these things, know that it is near—***at the doors***!" (Matthew 24:33, NKJV).
- "The master of that servant will come on a day when he is not looking for him and at an hour that ***he is not aware of***" (Matthew 24:50, NKJV).
- "That is the reason you should always *stay awake and be alert*, because you don't know the day or the hour when the Bridegroom will appear..." (Matthew 25:13, TPT).
- "***After a long time*** the lord of those servants came and settled accounts with them" (Matthew 25:19, NKJV).
- "***Watch and pray***, lest you enter into temptation" (Matthew 26:41, NKJV).
- "But ***stay awake*** at all times, praying that you may have strength to escape all these things that are going to take place, and to stand before the Son of Man" (Luke 21:36, ESV).
- "Take heed, ***watch and pray***; for you do not know when the time is" (Mark 13:33, NKJV).
- "***Watch*** therefore, for you do not know when the master of the house is coming—in the evening, at midnight, at the crowing of the rooster, or in the morning— lest, coming suddenly, he find you sleeping" (Mark 13:35-36, NKJV).
- "But know this, that if the master of the house had known what hour the thief would come, he would have watched and not

allowed his house to be broken into. Therefore you also ***be ready***, for the Son of Man is coming at an hour you do not expect" (Luke 12:39–40, NKJV).

- "The master of that servant ***will come on a day when he is not looking for him***, and at an hour when he is not aware, and will cut him in two and appoint him his portion with the unbelievers" (Luke 12:46, NKJV).
- "***Watch*** therefore, and pray always that you may be counted worthy to escape all these things that will come to pass, and to stand before the Son of Man" (Luke 21:36, NKJV).

These are the verses where Jesus personally directs the disciples to be watchful. In other words, to be alert, awake, and vigilant. I am not mentioning the many times the disciples wrote similarly to the churches.

To be alert or watchful does not mean to observe. In *Strong's Greek Lexicon* (G1127), "watch" means "to take heed lest through remission and indolence some destructive calamity suddenly overtakes one."[92]

Watch and pray. Always.

Jesus could not stress this point harder. In almost every parable about His coming, Jesus draws the same conclusion—you don't know when, so stay alert. His Bride will be ready, but will you be a part of it? What does it look like practically?

CHAPTER 13

REVIVAL LIFESTYLE

STAYING ALERT IS NOT A TOUGH BURDEN. It is a very lively state to be in. When you are alert, you are victorious.

You don't have to be a comfortable, foolish, sleeping, barren, or corrupt church. You can be so much more. You can be His Bride.

There is no need to overcomplicate things. It's quite simple. To be ready, you need to stay alert. In other words, living a revival lifestyle.

James Maloney writes, "The revival is a return to the basics; that sincere worship of God, that earnest relationship with Jesus, that pursuit of godly knowledge found in studying the Bible. All those things the apostles in the Book of Acts sought out, as well as the signs, wonders and miracles they saw, too."[93]

Staying alert means you are not comfortable. You are not passive or indifferent but passionate and radical. You don't rely on your own strength and never feel satisfied with where you are spiritually. You always crave more. "But you be watchful in all things, endure afflictions, do the work of an evangelist, fulfill your ministry" (2 Timothy 4:5, NKJV).

Staying alert means you know your Bible. You constantly feed on the truth, not the lies that come through the news, social media, gossip, and whatever else. You live by the Word and will not be deceived into the foolishness the Galatian's church fell into. "Therefore gird up the loins of your mind, be sober, and rest your hope fully upon the grace that is to be brought to you at the revelation of Jesus Christ" (1 Peter 1:13, NKJV).

Staying alert means you are not asleep. You are very much awake to the reality. You realize the time is short. You see all the massive events on a prophetic scale unfolding around the world. You can hear the footsteps of your Bridegroom. "Therefore let us not sleep, as others do, but let us watch and be sober" (1 Thessalonians 5:6, NKJV).

Staying alert means you are not barren. Before your eyes is only one vision, one mission, one desire—the person of Jesus Christ. You hold the Son of God as the dearest and the single most valuable possession. Nothing can replace Him. "Let your gentleness be known to all men. The Lord is at hand" (Philippians 4:5, NKJV).

Staying alert means you are not corrupt. You will never allow the rotting ways of the flesh to lead you. Instead, you live in constant surrender, walking by the Spirit. There is nothing that this world can offer you to bribe you out of spiritual effectiveness. "Watch, stand fast in the faith, be brave, be strong" (1 Corinthians 16:13, NKJV).

This is what makes up for the revival lifestyle we are called to live out. Pursue a relationship with Jesus, protect yourself from religion, and proclaim the Gospel in all regions. These will keep you sharp and strong.

Pursue a relationship with Jesus, protect yourself from religion, and proclaim the Gospel in all regions.

Make it your life's goal to ensure you are part of the Bride. Read Proverbs 31 often and keep aligning your lifestyle to that beautiful portrait. Pray to be like her, and you will never lose the wonder, the mystery, the love for Jesus Christ.

Much can still be said and added to this. I encourage you to keep digging into the end-time message. Always examine yourself. Be a voice of truth, not an echo of the culture. Be a healthy organ in the body of Christ—His church.

"Rejoice to the extent that you partake of Christ's sufferings, that when His glory is revealed, you may also be glad with exceeding joy" (1 Peter 4:13, NKJV).

Give me Jesus!
You can have all this world.
Give me Jesus!

ENDNOTES

1   Leonard Ravenhill. *Revival God's Way*. Page 126.

2   *The Passion Translation Bible*. Page 132.

3   Encounter Today (2023) Enoch's Lost Prophecy Uncovered—Pastor Alan DiDio, YouTube. Available at: https://www.youtube.com/watch?v=cDD1qB4VchU (Accessed: 30 October 2023).

4   *The Passion Translation Bible*. The Book of Genesis. Page 25.

5   The word between parenthesis was added by the author.

6   "Holy, Righteous Simeon the God-Receiver." www.oca.org. Retrieved April 27, 2023.

7   Revelation: The Seven Trumpets and When They Shall Sound (2014) Endtime Ministries. The Endtime Show. Available at: https://www.endtime.com/blog/revelation-seven-trumpets-shall-sound/?fbclid=IwAR2WwWvIlnqnNw-2ohbtC670NcJjW1PyqR0uPq_AeJVW-MqZZyXnT_4IFZKo (Accessed: 30 October 2023).

8   *The Passion Translation*. Page 996. Commentary for Proverbs 31:10.

9   James Maloney. *Ladies of Gold*. Volume 3. Page 42

10 "Church," noun—definition, pictures, pronunciation and usage notes ... (no date) Oxford Learner's Dictionary. Available at: https://www.oxfordlearnersdictionaries.com/definition/english/church (Accessed: 30 October 2023).

11 Francis Chan. *Crazy Love*. Page 203.

12 Benny Hinn. *The Blood*. Page 147.

13 Life Action Ministries | REVIVAL FORUM 1989. https://www.sermonindex.net/modules/newbb/viewtopic.php?topic_id=61164&forum=34

14 Leonard Ravenhill. *Why Revival Tarries*. Page 101.

15 Warren W. Wiersbe. *The Bible Exposition Commentary*. Page 580.

16 Warren W. Wiersbe. *The Bible Exposition Commentary*. Page 580.

17 Vance Havner. *Repent or Else*. Page 86, 88.

18 Warren W. Wiersbe. *The Bible Exposition Commentary*. Volume 2. Page 580.

19 Warren W. Wiersbe. *The Bible Exposition Commentary*. Page 581.

20 Vance Havner. *Three-Score & Ten*.

21 Bethel Music. "Seas of Crimson." On We Will Not Be Shaken. Bethel Music, 2015.

22 Johnson, B. (2015) Bill Johnson: Going Face to Face with God—Charisma Magazine Online, Charisma Magazine Online—The Magazine About Spirit-led Living. Available at: https://mycharisma.com/spiritled-living/supernaturaldreams/going-face-to-face-with-god/ (Accessed: 30 October 2023).

23 Leonard Ravenhill. *Why Revival Tarries*. Page 101.

24 Paul David Tripp. *Dangerous Calling*. Page 195.

25 Drs. Jerry & Carol Robeson. *Strongman's His Name... What's His Game?* Page 57.

26 Leonard Ravenhill. *Revival God's Way*. Page 52.

27 Reiland, D. (no date) How Much Money Should Your Church Spend and on What?, CFaith. Available at: https://www.cfaith.com/index.php/blog/38-articles/

ENDNOTES

ministry/15860-how-much-money-should-your-church-spend-and-on-what (Accessed: 30 October 2023).

28 Maxwell, P. (2019) How Churches Really Spend Their Money: 20 Fascinating Data Points [A New Study], Thite.ly. Available at: https://get.tithe.ly/blog/how-churches-really-spend-their-money-20-fascinating-data-points-a-new-study (Accessed: 30 October 2023).

29 Wei, J. (2023) Don't Tell Me Where Your Priorities Are—James W. Frick, Due. Available at: https://due.com/dont-tell-me-where-your-priorities-are-james-w-frick/ (Accessed: 30 October 2023).

30 Foster, D. (2023) How Churches Really Spend Their Money, Medium. Available at: https://medium.com/backyard-theology/how-churches-really-spend-their-money-93195ae92ce3 (Accessed: 30 October 2023).

31 Robby Dawkins. *Identity Thief*. Page 211–212.

32 Derek Prince (no date). Picture 2: The Body: Podcast: Derek Prince Ministries, Podcast | Derek Prince Ministries. Available at: https://www.derekprince.com/radio/654 (Accessed: 30 October 2023).

33 Descyple91 (2012) Vance Havner—Three temptations of the Church, YouTube. Available at: https://www.youtube.com/watch?v=VpvR2gg1c9s (Accessed: 30 October 2023).

34 God Has Not Passed You By | worldchallenge.org (no date) World Challenge. Available at: https://www.worldchallenge.org/god-has-not-passed-you (Accessed: 30 October 2023).

35 Derek Prince. (no date b) Sin, Righteousness, Judgment: Sermon: Derek Prince Ministries, Sermon | Derek Prince Ministries. Available at: https://www.derekprince.com/sermons/35 (Accessed: 30 October 2023).

36 iThink Biblically. (2022) Leonard Ravenhill | Sermon Jam | Are You Dead to Sin or Dead in Sin? YouTube. Available at: https://www.youtube.com/watch?v=raZgxsBOOxM (Accessed: 04 December 2023).

37 Mark Sayers. *Reappearing Church*. Page 188.

38 Savchuk, V. (2020) 7. Why Discipleship Is the Solution for Pandemic and Persecution (Jason Lozano), YouTube. Available at: https://youtu.be/WlioSbOWK3I?si=oORHbkwqpJc5-Tjj (Accessed: 30 October 2023).

39 Derek Prince. *Shaping History Through Prayer and Fasting*. Page 30

40 Modeling the Future of Religion in America (2022) Pew Research Center's Religion & Public Life Project. Available at: https://www.pewresearch.org/religion/2022/09/13/modeling-the-future-of-religion-in-america/ (Accessed: 30 October 2023).

41 Foust, M. (2022) "Shocking" New Poll: Only 37 Percent of U.S. Pastors Hold a Biblical Worldview, ChristianHeadlines.com. Available at: https://www.christianheadlines.com/contributors/michael-foust/shocking-new-poll-only-37-percent-of-us-pastors-hold-a-biblical-worldview.html (Accessed: 30 October 2023).

42 Quintanilla, M. (2022) Survey: More than 1/3 of Senior Pastors Believe Being a "Good Person" Can Earn You Salvation, ChristianHeadlines.com. Available at: https://www.christianheadlines.com/contributors/milton-quintanilla/survey-more-than-1-3-of-senior-pastors-believe-being-a-good-person-can-earn-you-salvation.html (Accessed: 30 October 2023).

43 James Maloney. *The Dancing Hand of God*. Volume 2. Page 39

44 Maril Murillo. *Vessels of Fire & Glory*. Page 81

45 Paul David Tripp. *Dangerous Calling*. Page 73

46 Leonard Ravenhill. *Sodom Had No Bible*. Page 35.

47 Bob Larson. *Larson's Book on Spiritual Warfare*. Page 281.

48 Bob Larson. *Larson's Book on Spiritual Warfare*. Page 281.

49 Johnson, J. (2023) The Arm of the Flesh in America!, YouTube. Available at: https://youtu.be/QyQ9ZQxDXtM?si=sAXDv5FJpslX-FEa3 (Accessed: 30 October 2023).

50 Mario Murillo. *Vessels of Fire & Glory*. Page 50.

51 Leonard Ravenhill. *Why Revival Tarries*. Page 137.

52 James Maloney. *Ladies of Gold*. Page 172.

ENDNOTES

53 *The Passion Translation Bible.* Acts 20:9
54 Words between parenthesis added by the author.
55 Mario Murillo. *Vessels of Fire & Glory.* Page 45.
56 Carlos Sarmiento. *Encountered by God.* Pages 31–32.
57 Mario Murillo. *Vessels of Fire & Glory.* Page 16.
58 Kris Vallotton. *Poverty, Riches & Wealth.* Page 41.
59 Kris Vallotton. *Poverty, Riches & Wealth.*
60 Mario Murillo. *Edgewise.* Page 86.
61 Paul David Tripp. *Dangerous Calling.* Page 52.

62 Robby Dawkins. *Do What Jesus Did: A Real-Life Field Guide to Healing the Sick, Routing Demons and Changing Lives Forever.*

63 Robby Dawkins. *Do What Jesus Did: A Real-Life Field Guide to Healing the Sick, Routing Demons and Changing Lives Forever.* Page 27.

64 Robby Dawkins. *Do What Jesus Did: A Real-Life Field Guide to Healing the Sick, Routing Demons and Changing Lives Forever.*

65 R. T. Kendall. *Pigeon Religion.* Page 4.

66 Drs. Jerry & Carol Robeson. *Strongman's His Name... What's His Game?* Page 49.

67 James Maloney. *The Dancing Hand of God.* Volume 2. Page 173.
68 Mark Sayers. *Disappearing Church.* Page 31.
69 Mark Sayers. *Disappearing Church.* Page 34.
70 Mark Sayers. *Disappearing Church.* Page 37.

71 *Morning and Evening,* Based on the English Standard Version by Charles Haddon Spurgeon.

72 Have You Felt Like Giving Up Lately? Finding Hope and Healing When You Feel Discouraged (ed. Baker Books, 2012)—ISBN: 9781441240491.

73 Bob Larson. *Larson's Book of Spiritual Warefare.* Page 190.

74 Dr. J. Vernon McGee. *Chapter IV: The Three Entrances: The Doctrine of Worship.*

75 Dr. J. Vernon McGee: *Chapter IV: The Three Entrances: The Doctrine of Worship.*

76 Francis Chan. *Letters to the Church.*

77 Derek Prince (no date) True and False Church—Part 1: Sermon: Derek Prince Ministries, Sermon | Derek Prince Ministries. Available at: https://www.derekprince.com/sermons/419 (Accessed: 30 October 2023).

78 Kenneth E. Hagin. *The Believer's Authority.* Page 3.

79 Leonard Ravenhill. *Why Revival Tarries.* Page 60.

80 Leonard Ravenhill. *Why Revival Tarries.*

81 Mario Murillo. *Vessels of Fire & Glory.* Page 89.

82 Shawn Bolz. *Exploring the Prophetic.* Page 20.

83 James Maloney. *The Dancing Hand of God.* Volume 2. Page 62

84 James Maloney. *Ladies of Gold.* Volume 1. Page 76.

85 Mario Murillo. *Vessels of Fire & Glory.* Page 13.

86 Derek Prince (no date) You Also Must Be Ready: Sermon: Derek Prince Ministries, Sermon | Derek Prince Ministries. Available at: https://www.derekprince.com/sermons/4 (Accessed: 30 October 2023).

87 Mark Sayers. *Reappearing Church.* Page 126.

88 Derek Prince (no date) The Bride Prepares Herself: Sermon: Derek Prince Ministries, Sermon | Derek Prince Ministries. Available at: https://www.derekprince.com/sermons/37 (Accessed: 30 October 2023).

89 Derek Prince (no date) The Church: Sermon: Derek Prince Ministries, Sermon | Derek Prince Ministries. Available at: https://www.derekprince.com/sermons/221 (Accessed: 30 October 2023).

90 Life Center Ministries (2023) Sunday Morning || 11am (EST) service || Randy Clark, YouTube. Available at: https://www.youtube.com/watch?v=cBsbXBNqdkQ (Accessed: 30 October 2023).

91 Mark Sayers. Reappearing Church. Page 95.

92 Blue Letter Bible (no date) G1127—*Grēgoreō*—Strong's Greek Lexicon (KJV). Available at: https://www.blueletterbible.org/lexicon/g1127/kjv/tr/0-1/ (Accessed: 28 December 2023).

93 James Maloney. *The Dancing Hand of God*. Volume 2. Page 281.

Printed in the USA
CPSIA information can be obtained
at www.ICGtesting.com
LVHW010738060324
773637LV00004B/8